The Spiritual Journey

Becoming One with Christ in Divine Love

JOSEPH GELAK

WESTBOW
PRESS®
A DIVISION OF THOMAS NELSON
& ZONDERVAN

WestBow Press books may be ordered through booksellers or by contacting:

WestBow Press
A Division of Thomas Nelson & Zondervan
1663 Liberty Drive
Bloomington, IN 47403
www.westbowpress.com
1 (866) 928-1240

ISBN: 978-1-9736-5225-0 (sc)
ISBN: 978-1-9736-5227-4 (hc)
ISBN: 978-1-9736-5226-7 (e)

Library of Congress Control Number: 2019901100

Print information available on the last page.

WestBow Press rev. date: 1/31/2019

Dedicated to my parents who showed me that God is worth pursuing, to my lovely wife Deanna for her patience and kindness, for our children Tiffany and Andrew who are an encouragement to me and light up my life, and for our international student Grace who blesses us more than she knows and shows us what real faith looks like.

With great appreciation for my editor, Brittany Clarke. She exemplifies professional excellence with the love of Christ shining through.

Contents

Introduction

The idea of the journey is embedded deep in the human psyche.

We love to read about journeys—*The Epic of Gilgamesh*, the oldest known work of fiction; *Odyssey* by Homer; *The Lord of the Rings* by J.R.R. Tolkien; *The Lion, the Witch and the Wardrobe* by C.S. Lewis; and *The Wizard of Oz* by L. Frank Baum, to name just a few. All of these feature great and heroic journeys. Or in real life, we enjoy hearing about the travels of David Livingstone in Africa from 1851–1873 and the 13th-century voyage of Marco Polo from Italy through Asia to the Orient and back.

One of the most interesting journeys in history was one made by Rabbi Benjamin of Tudela. Rabbi Benjamin left his home in Tudela, in northern Spain, in 1168 AD. He traveled far and wide to check on the many dispersed communities of Jews found in Europe and Asia and North Africa. His journey took place at a time when the old Roman road system was falling apart, transportation was slow and difficult, the land between cities was littered with marauding bandits, and the seas were crisscrossed by pirates ready to relieve travelers of their property and sometimes their lives as well.

Rabbi Benjamin and his small group of three companions traveled far and wide, covering areas of modern day Egypt, France, Italy,

Greece, Turkey, Lebanon, Israel, Iraq, Iran, and Saudi Arabia. He viewed such amazing sites, beyond Rome and Constantinople (Istanbul) and many other cities, as the sepulchre of King Uzziah; the pillar of salt into which Lot's wife was turned (which he says the sheep licked continually); the sepulchres of the House of David and the sepulchres of the kings who ruled after him; the house of Abraham; the ruins of Nineveh; the synagogue of Obadiah in Assur (Mosul), reputedly built by Jonah; the ruins of Babylon that extended 30 miles in length; the ruins of the palace of Nebuchadnezzar; the "furnace into which were thrown Hananiah, Mishael, and Azariah"; the sepulchre of Daniel; and the ruins of the Tower of Babel, which he describes as follows:

> The length of its foundation is about two miles, the breadth of the tower is about forty cubits, and the length there of two hundred cubits. At every ten cubits' distance there are slopes which go round the tower by which one can ascend to the top. One can see from there a view twenty miles in extent, as the land is level.[1]

Amazing!

What is it about journeys that capture our dreams and imagination? It might be the excitement of adventure, escaping beyond the mundane. It might be that we have a need for transcendence, something bigger than ourselves. It might be the need to overcome obstacles and challenges. It might be that the journey imparts to us a greater vision and understanding of life. In the end result, often more important than reaching the destination, is that the traveler is changed. As travelers, we can be transformed all the way down into our souls, our inner beings.

---

[1] Benjamin of Tuleda, *The Itinerary of Benjamin of Tudela* (1907).

What sort of journey achieves all of this and fulfills us forever? Only one journey—the one God has planned and intended for each one of us. We need to know that God has something different for us than what we are today. He will change us and transform us in amazing ways. He promises to bring us safely through the journey if we follow him faithfully.

This purpose of this book is to explore this magnificent journey that God has designed for us.

If you are skeptical of spiritual matters

If you have doubts of God's existence, or whether he is involved and cares about you, or if he is willing and able to help, I have no array of arguments, facts, and reasoning to share here except this: I believe the journey described herein has been proven by the real-life experiences of many persons from many places down throughout the ages. Can I suggest that this journey works because it is true, and it is true because it works? What is there to risk on such a journey but what is temporary anyway?

Chapter 1

Our Journey's Destination – Oneness with Christ

Each creature God made must live in its own true nature;
How could I resist my nature, that lives for oneness with God?
—Mechthild of Magdeburg

As the cliché goes, we need to start with the end in mind. What is the destination of our spiritual journey?

Have you considered what in life is so significant that it should dominate absolutely everything—our thoughts, our dreams, our feelings, our time, our energy, our passion? So significant that it is worthy of our continuous seeking and pursuit? What we truly yearn for and desire, whether we are fully conscious of it or not?

This gets interesting because Jesus is not only our Good Shepherd who empowers and helps us complete our journey. He is also our destination!

This is the one such thing. It is God's design for us to become one with him in Christ. It is far beyond what we can even ask for or imagine. It is beyond all words and thoughts and concepts. It is the fulfillment and completion that is meant for us.

If you know this and you are on the journey, wonderful. But for many of us it can seem somehow foreign and alien. Or impossibly distant and unachievable. This may be true regardless of our spiritual or religious backgrounds and beliefs, and regardless of our current spiritual practices and activities. But we can know and have assurance it is real, it is achievable in Christ, and it is the end state of our spiritual journey.

How do we know this is true?

If we are to consider dedicating our lives to this journey to oneness with Christ, it seems only fair to have some confidence that it is indeed God's will and plan for us, and that this state of oneness with Christ really exists.

We can be thankful that God makes it very clear in his Word that this is his will and design and plan and intended destiny for us:

> Therefore if you have any encouragement from being united with Christ . . . (Philippians 2:1)

> . . . we will certainly also be united with him in a resurrection like his. (Romans 6:5)

> Therefore, there is now no condemnation for those who are in Christ Jesus, (Romans 8:1)

> For in him we live and move and have our being. (Acts 17:28)

. . . he made known to us the mystery of his will . . .
to bring unity to all things in heaven and on earth
under Christ. (Ephesians 1:9–10)

I am the vine; you are the branches. If you remain
in me and I in you, you will bear much fruit. . .
(John 15:5)

But whoever is united with the Lord is one with
him in spirit. (1 Corinthians 6:17)

It is because of him [God] that you are in Christ
Jesus, (1 Corinthians 1:30)

Before long, the world will not see me anymore,
but you will see me. Because I live, you also will
live. On that day you will realize that I am in my
Father, and you are in me, and I am in you. (John
14:19–20)

Note that most of the verses listed are in present tense. They apply
to this life, not just after physical death. We may hope that we
will physically die and end up in heaven, but there is more. God's
plan is that we first spiritually enter and dwell in heaven in Christ
before our physical death!

How do we know this? Because ". . . God raised us up with Christ
and seated us with him in the heavenly realms in Christ Jesus"
(Ephesians 2:6).

What is this oneness?

Many of us have probably heard these verses on being one with Christ many times. But have we really stopped and thought about what oneness with him really means? What does "being united" with, or "in" Christ, look like? Feel like?

What comes to your mind when you think of oneness with Christ? Contemplate this for a moment.

What is it like to experience oneness with Christ? I went for so long without a clue. It is probably different for each person. Of course, it cannot be expressed satisfactorily in words. To be fully known and understood, it must be experienced personally.

> *And if you should want to hear:*
> *this highest knowledge lies*
> *in the loftiest sense*
> *of the essence of God;*
> *this is a work of his mercy…*
> *transcending all knowledge.*
> —St. John of the Cross, A Gloss

However, maybe we can get some inkling of what oneness with Christ is like from someone else's account. Here is how one anonymous person described their encounter with God when he or she experienced a near death experience:

> The white light of His penetrating energy was unstoppable. It couldn't be dimmed. It touched me and went deeper still, beneath my physical self, of whom only a perception remained. His vast, white presence, soaked into every part of me, diving deep into my core and stealing my breath,

of which I had no need, because I was filled with His light. I lay myself bare to this energy, letting it fill every empty place inside me. It took up all those spaces without diminishing me in any way, for the white energy of God does not take from us, it only gives . . . filling us to overflowing.

And here are two more brief testimonies to the power and greatness of the experience:

A Light of utmost splendor glows on the eyes of my soul. Therein have I seen the inexpressible ordering of all things, and recognized God's unspeakable glory – that incomprehensible wonder – the tender caress between God and the soul . . . the unmingled joy of union, the living love of eternity as it now is and evermore shall be.[2]

This spiritual delight we cannot imagine no matter how hard we try. It is fashioned from the purest gold of Divine Wisdom.[3]

Sublime

There is perhaps also another way of acquiring a small sense of the wonderful greatness of being one in Christ. Here is how.

---

[2] Mechthild of Magdeburg
[3] Teresa of Avila

Something is said to be sublime when it is of such excellence, grandeur, or beauty as to inspire great admiration or awe.[4] What is sublime is perhaps a taste of the nature of God.

Think back to a time when you had such an experience. A wonderful memory. It may have been a work of art—a painting, a photograph, a song, a piece of literature. It may have been God's beauty in creation—a waterfall, a mountain, the shining sea, an animal or plant. It may have been an athletic or acrobatic act of great strength and skill. It may have been the discovery of a concept in science or mathematics.

Whatever it is for you, consider that it is a tiny foretaste of the greatness, beauty, and nature of God, for "The heavens declare the glory of God; the skies proclaim the work of his hands" (Psalm 19:1). Since we are created in God's image and everything is from him, all we in turn create that is beautiful reflects something of his nature.

Perhaps we were given these experiences for this very purpose, to give us a hint. From this we can realize that God has designed us to partake in his fullness and his nature and attributes that these experiences in some small way remind us of. We can thank him for such experiences, that they might inspire and motivate us to pursue him.

Contemplation: Is this destination of union with Christ in divine love something that you want and desire above all things?

---

[4] "sublime, adj.1". OED Online. December 2018. Oxford University Press. https://en.oxforddictionaries.com/definition/sublime (accessed January 01, 2019).

*Whereas the beautiful is limited, the sublime is limitless,
so that the mind in the presence of the sublime, attempting
to imagine what it cannot, has pain in the failure but
pleasure in contemplating the immensity of the attempt.*
—Immanuel Kant, *Critique of Pure Reason*

*When I look out on such a night as this, I feel as if there
could be neither wickedness nor sorrow in the world; and
there certainly would be less of both if the sublimity of
Nature were more attended to, and people were carried
more out of themselves by contemplating such a scene.*
—Jane Austen

Oneness

Oneness is the union with Christ in divine love. Francis of Assisi describes it this way:

> The tree of love its roots hath spread
> Deep in my heart, and rears its head;
> Rich are its fruits: they joy dispense;
> Transport the heart, and ravish sense.
> In love's sweet swoon to thee I cleave,
> Bless'd source of love.

God is perfect love. We can become one with God in Christ through the union of perfect, divine love. For Christ loves us with a deep and everlasting and unconditional love, perfected and proven by great sacrifice:

> . . . as Christ also loved you and gave Himself up
> for us . . . (Ephesians 5:2)

> This is how we know what love is: Jesus Christ laid down his life for us. And we ought to lay down our lives for our brothers and sisters. (1 John 3:16)

> . . . may have power, together with all the Lord's holy people, to grasp how wide and long and high and deep is the love of Christ, and to know this love that surpasses knowledge—that you may be filled to the measure of all the fullness of God. (Ephesians 3:18–19)

It is a beautiful thing. It is also wonderful that his love is not dependent on anything. It is not dependent on our being "lovely" or performing well or somehow being worthy of his love. We can venture to say that he did not even need to decide to love us. Why? Because he is love in his very substance. This is his nature; this is what he is. "God is love" (1 John 4:16).

We can be thankful to God that he opens the door and provides us with a way to achieve this oneness with Christ. He will give us what we need for the journey. He will guide us and protect us and provide for us and strengthen us so as to make it possible. He will be our faithful traveling companion; "he will never leave you nor forsake you" (Deuteronomy 31:6).

Nothing is sweeter than love, nothing stronger, nothing higher, nothing wider, nothing more pleasant, nothing fuller or better in heaven or earth; for love is born of God, and can rest only in God above all created things.
—Thomas a Kempis

Jesus, draw me into the flames of your love . . . Unite me so closely with you that you live and act in me.
—Thérèse de Lisieux

Chapter 2

Separated from God

If God's design for us is to be one with him in Christ, then why did we wake up this morning not as one with him?

Because we became separated from God. We left him. We departed from the one who loves us. Jesus expresses it so well in what we often call the story of the prodigal son:

> There was a man who had two sons. The younger one said to his father, "Father, give me my share of the estate." So he divided his property between them.
>
> Not long after that, the younger son got together all he had, set off for a distant country. (Luke 15:11–13)

Here is a father who loved his son. But his son wanted to break out on his own. He had his own agenda, his own desires, his own ambitions. He wanted to experience what he had never experienced. So, he left and traveled to a far country.

Jesus tells this to depict our relationship with God. Our God is at home; we are in "the far country." We will explore this story more later since it is key to our spiritual journey.

> *God is always ready,*
> *but we are very unready;*
> *God is near to us,*
> *but we are far from Him;*
> *God is within, but we are without;*
> *God is at home, but we are strangers.*
> —Meister Eckhart, "God is Always Ready"

How separation from God started

We were not the first to separate from God. Satan, or the devil, did so first, and many angels followed him. Whatever your belief is concerning Satan, the important thing is to understand certain things that are said about him, since they will shed light on how we became separated from God.

Satan started well, with the name Lucifer. In Latin, Lucifer means "light-bringing." He originally may have helped channel and bring light into heaven. But he decided he was too good for a support role and wanted to supplant God. God says this about him:

> You said in your heart,
> "I will ascend to the heavens;
> I will raise my throne
> above the stars of God;
> I will sit enthroned on the mount of assembly,
> on the utmost heights of Mount Zaphon.
> I will ascend above the tops of the clouds;
> I will make myself like the Most High."
> (Isaiah 14:13–14)

There is only one God, so this cannot be. That is why Satan fell, as described in Revelation 12:9:

> The great dragon was hurled down—that ancient serpent called the devil, or Satan, who leads the whole world astray. He was hurled to the earth, and his angels with him.

In the Garden of Eden

Now we turn to the story of humanity. You are probably familiar with the story of Adam and Eve and the garden and the serpent (Satan) and the apple. The story is found in Genesis 3. We will just summarize here.

Whatever you believe about the literal accuracy of this story is not so important. What is important for our spiritual journey is that it contains powerful truth that will prove to be very helpful. For this reason, we will refer backward to the garden many times as we move forward.

According to the story, humanity first lived in what is called the Garden of Eden. It is thought by some to be located somewhere in what is now modern-day Iraq.

The idea of life in the garden before sin entered in is one of idyllic peace and serenity. It is pictured as plush, abundant with trees and fruit, and teeming with cool, refreshing streams and fountains and animals coexisting in peace.

God instructed Adam and Eve as follows for their good:

> You are free to eat from any tree in the garden; but you must not eat from the tree of the knowledge of good and evil, for when you eat from it you will certainly die. (Genesis 2:16–17)

Now Satan, the devil, took the form of a serpent (later depicted as a dragon) and showed up to tempt and trick humanity:

> He [Satan] said to the woman, "Did God really say, 'You must not eat from any tree in the garden'?"
>
> The woman said to the serpent, "We may eat fruit from the trees in the garden, but God did say, 'You must not eat fruit from the tree that is in the middle of the garden, and you must not touch it, or you will die.'"
>
> "You will not certainly die," the serpent said to the woman. "For God knows that when you eat from it your eyes will be opened, and you will be like God, knowing good and evil."
>
> When the woman saw that the fruit of the tree was good for food and pleasing to the eye, and also desirable for gaining wisdom, she took some and ate it. She also gave some to her husband, who was with her, and he ate it. (Genesis 3:1–6)

It is interesting how this correlates with Satan's fall. Satan was "in Eden, the garden of God" (Ezekiel 28:13). Satan said, "I will make myself like the Most High,"; and now he tells humanity, "you will be like God." God said to him, "you corrupted your wisdom" (Ezekiel 28:17); Satan promises that we will know good from evil, and humanity believes the fruit is "desirable for gaining wisdom." God said to Satan "Your heart was proud because of your beauty,"; and humanity is attracted to the fruit partly because it is "pleasing to the eye."

In short, we followed Satan in his separation from God. We sinned. We acted outside of the will of God. By our actions in the garden, we severed our love relationship with God. This is what we call "the fall." God is on high. He is above all things. While we were connected with him, he upheld us and sustained us with him in a higher place. But now the relationship severed, so we fell. We broke the attachments we had with God.

Attachments

The concept of attachments plays a big part in our spiritual journey to oneness with Christ. We can view an attachment as a connection between us and something else.

God is self-existent and self-sufficient and complete in himself. He needs nothing and is dependent on nothing outside himself.

We are different. God created us. As created beings, we are not self-existent and self-sufficient and complete. Some of what we are dependent on is very evident—oxygen, water, food, shelter. Some things are more intangible—the need for attention, affirmation, love, significance, and success, for example.

To understand the fall, we need to understand how our attachments changed. In the garden we had attachments, such as to the fruit from the trees, air, soil, streams of water, and light. However, for the sake of our spiritual journey, the Genesis story is not really about the physical creation of the cosmos and the earth and biological life on the earth. It is about spiritual realities. It represents the relationship we had with God. When we realize this it all begins to make sense.

God designed our one true macro, over-arching attachment to be our perfect divine love with him. Think of this love as the sun. The sun expresses itself to us, interacts with us, reaches us, impacts us, and communicates with us in a sense, through its beams of light, its photons, which are transmitted from the sun to our planet. We then receive the sun through perceptions of light received in our eyes and the feeling of warmth on our skin.

In the garden, the fruit, the water, and the light represent the expressions and manifestations of God's divine love. These are the attachments, the connections, that we needed, received, and enjoyed and that caused us to flourish. These divine attachments flow from and through Christ and through the Spirit of God. This is why Jesus called himself our manna, or bread (food), from heaven (John 6:35) and our light of the world. (8:12) He offers to give us living waters (4:10) and spiritual air to breathe, both of which are his Spirit. (living waters represent God's Spirit in John 7:37-39; and both the Hebrew term "ruah" and the Greek term "pneuma" are used for the Holy Spirit (when capitalized) and breath.

When our love relationship with God was severed by our doing, we lost these wonderful attachments.

The Curse

Since the garden was our divine love relationship with God, we lost it once we broke the relationship. In the Word of God it was described as our exile from God: "So the Lord God banished him

[Adam] from the Garden of Eden" (Genesis 3:23). The exile, or our banishment from the garden, was not necessarily so much a change of physical location as a change of condition and being. We were banished from the garden to the land east of Eden (Genesis 3:24). Life would be very different in our exile. Our new life conditions are commonly called "the curse."

This curse is not what we may typically think of as a curse. It was not profanity or profane. It was not condemnation. I think of it as proclaiming the unavoidable consequences of our actions.

We brought the exile upon ourselves, by our thoughts and decisions and actions. We therefore swapped the attachments we had in the garden for vastly inferior attachments.

We decided God had not been fully truthful with us regarding his instructions that we avoid eating the fruit of the tree of the knowledge of good and evil. We listened to the lie of the enemy instead. Ever since, we have a tendency to believe the lies of the enemy.

We betrayed God, the one we owed everything to, at the very moment when we gained the knowledge of good and evil. This resulted in guilt, shame, and the need to justify ourselves, defend ourselves, and blame our circumstances and others.

We wanted to become like God, so we incurred an insatiable need for power, control, prominence, and significance. We therefore took a position of independence from God, causing separation.

We crossed the boundary to enjoy the pleasure of forbidden fruit— "good for food and pleasing to the eye." By doing so, we decided that the provision of God, all of the other fruit, was not sufficient. We needed more. We are now continuously seeking new pleasures and entertainment and thrills, regardless of the price we must pay to do so. This includes but goes far beyond the lusts of the flesh. It includes needing to feel more successful and more significant and more productive and more responsible and more accomplished, things that are deemed good.

By the fruit in the garden we participated in and received the qualities of God. Now we must scratch in the ground for an inferior food that is not satisfying and leaves us wanting.

By losing access to the tree of life found in the center of the garden, our spiritual life and vitality ran out, leaving us "dead" in our sins (Ephesians 2:1). In short, we were alienated and separated from God.

This is the curse that is often referred to in Scripture. The curse plays out in constant struggle and strife, ending in death.

Inner place and outer place

Throughout Scripture there is a recurring idea of there being an "inner place" where God is found and an "outer place" of our exile that is distant and separated from God. The garden story portrays this dichotomy. Humanity was cast out from the safety and beauty of the garden to the land east of Eden with its struggles and suffering.

Scripture is also replete with many other examples. Inside the ark sheltering Noah and the flood waters outside. The Promised Land and the outside nations. The city of Jerusalem and other cities. Inside the Ark of the Covenant and outside of it. Inside the temple and outside the temple. Inside the city of God and outside in the city of man.

This encompassing truth in Scripture points to what is also true in our lives. We as individuals have an inner being and an outer being.

Our inner being is referred to as our soul. It is our true self as God intended it to be. It is where we are designed to connect with God. It is like a room or space where we go to meet him. It is the deepest part of us, our essence. It is eternal.

Demonstrating the parallel in Scripture, our inner being is depicted as a garden:

> And you will be like a watered garden,
> You will be like a well-watered garden,
> like a spring whose waters never fail. (Isaiah 58:11)

In contrast, our outer being is the part of us that interacts with the world around us and outside of us. It is not just our physical existence. It is the life in this world—our education, our responsibilities, our circumstances, our money, our relationships with people, our society, and our culture. All that is outside of our souls.

As a result of the curse we brought on ourselves and our exile from the garden, the outer world now dominates our focus and efforts and attention and desires. We have been cast into our outer being in a sense. Our time, our energy, our efforts, our hopes and dreams, and our measure of success are now typically centered around all the things in our outer being.

This goes far beyond the need for survival in the physical world. Our inner efforts—our dreams and imagination and desires and purposes—which should be directed toward connecting us with God, are now instead focused on our outer being. Since we have lost God, our outer being requires endless striving and struggle in a vain attempt to obtain what is missing. Our outer being is now viewed as the only thing that is "real." Our outer being with its constant demands and near total dominance over us is now what we call the "self." It is what produces selfishness and self-interest and self-seeking and self-indulgence and self-righteousness.

Consequently, sometimes our true inner being, our soul as God designed it, seems hidden and invisible.

Where does our spiritual journey take place?

The spiritual journey that God has for us is to happen in our souls, in our inner being:

> Jesus said, "Neither shall they say, Lo here! or, lo there! for, behold, the kingdom of God is within you". (Luke 17:21 KJV)

> The soul is joined with Him in the dwelling places very close to the center while the mind may be on the outskirts of the castle suffering from a thousand wild poisonous beasts,
> —Teresa of Avila

It is where we are destined to become one with God, if we pursue the spiritual journey he has designed for us.

> The Lord showed me, so that I did see clearly, that he did not dwell in these temples which men had commanded and set up, but in people's hearts . . . his people were his temple, and he dwelt in them.
> —George Fox, founder of the Quakers

We know that God has a heart that desires to dwell in us:

> I stand at the door and knock. If anyone hears
> my voice and opens the door, I will come in . . .
> (Revelation 3:20)

We might view our inner being like the ocean. Humanity originally knew, experienced, and perceived very little of the ocean below the surface. But then greater exploration gradually revealed an immense world of life and complexity and diversity and adventure under the sea. With our souls it is similar. What is in us must not only be explored, but also created and grown.

The desire in our souls for God is also a sort of yearning, a type of remembering or reawakening. It is as if we were banged over the head and have amnesia. Suddenly our phone rings and we answer it. We hear the voice on the other end. We cannot call to mind exactly who it is or how we know the person, yet the unmistakable feeling comes over us that they are familiar to us and we know them. We have a sense that they are near and dear to us, that they play a key role in our life. The more time we spend with them and look at them and talk with them the more we remember and our life returns. This is like our relationship with Jesus.

> *God is more interior to us than we are to ourselves.*
> *His acting in us is nearer and more inward than our own actions.*
> *God works in us from inside outwards;*
> *creatures work on us from the outside.*
> —John of Ruysbroeck, *Spiritual Espousals, complete works*

Chapter 3

Our Good Shepherd's Map

God has a unique spiritual journey planned for each of us. There are as many different journeys as there are different people. We can see from his Word how each person has a unique story—Noah, Abraham, Jacob, Joseph, Moses, Ruth, Jonah, Jesus, and Paul, just to name a few.

Yet at the same time there are some things that are common across every journey. There are universal elements that determine the success of the journey. That is why we can be confident that God has a map for our journey. It reveals where he is headed and how we are to follow.

The map is found in his Word. It is found throughout scripture. Here is what the Psalmist, King David, beautifully said about his journey with the Shepherd in Psalm 23:

The Lord is my shepherd, I lack nothing.
He makes me lie down in green pastures,
he leads me beside quiet waters,
he refreshes my soul.
He guides me along the right paths
for his name's sake.
Even though I walk
through the darkest valley,
I will fear no evil,
for you are with me;
your rod and your staff,
they comfort me.
You prepare a table before me
in the presence of my enemies.
You anoint my head with oil;
my cup overflows.
Surely your goodness and love will follow me
all the days of my life,
and I will dwell in the house of the Lord
forever.

Thanks to God; he wants to lead us, help us, and empower us. But we need to understand how, so that we can respond and cooperate with him and do our part. We must know what our Good Shepherd is up to, where he is headed, and how we can follow. It is like a dance. Jesus is leading. We can successfully follow his lead.

God wants us to know the map intimately so that we can successfully end up at our destination, entirely fulfilled in Christ's divine love. The map reveals the major elements of the journey. These are:

Calling us.
Providing for us.

Leading us.
Testing us.
Redeeming us.

We will go through each of these together in the following chapters.

Phase One: Calling Us

The Good Shepherd finds us far from the true path, wandering. Isaiah 53:6 says, "We all, like sheep, have gone astray, each of us has turned to our own way." He calls to us, and we must make the decision to listen, respond to, and follow the Shepherd. This is when we say with conviction and passion, "The Lord is my Shepherd" (Psalm 23:1).

We are never too far from him such that he would balk at finding us or decide we are not worthy of his time. The distance, and our condition, is never a problem for him. He specializes in finding those who are most lost. His eyes are upon us even now. He sees all and knows all and yet still loves us beyond all comprehension.

How should we respond? Not by some heroic deed performed in our own strength. Not in shame and guilt. Not with apathy or coldness.

We should respond in a way that is fitting of that which is being offered to us, the experience of being one in perfect love with the God of all. We should respond with openness and surrender, with appreciation, in awe and wonder.

Chapter 4

A Way for Our Return

Thankfully our separation from God does not need to be permanent! While God announced our banishment from the garden, he has spent the rest of history graciously working to undo the curse and reconcile with us. He wants us back.

We can view our separation from God as something we must necessarily pass through to get to the other side and be restored. God's Word depicts it as passing through the night to get to the morning, and enduring the winter to get to spring. For this is God's promise:

> weeping may stay for the night,
> but rejoicing comes in the morning.
> (Psalm 30:5)

It is as Solomon writes: "See! The winter is past; the rains are over and gone. Flowers appear on the earth; the season of singing has come" (Song of Solomon 2:11–12). God's solution is for us to undergo a spiritual journey back to him through Christ.

We can know this is in the heart of God since his Word gives us stories of separation, exile, and return. One of these stories is a precursor to the story of the prodigal son. It features King Nebuchadnezzar, the head of the Babylonian Empire around the 7th century BC, who is believed to have built the famous Hanging Gardens of Babylon. Here is how it begins:

> . . . as the king was walking on the roof of the royal palace of Babylon, he said, "Is not this the great Babylon I have built as the royal residence, by my mighty power and for the glory of my majesty?" (Daniel 4:29–30)

Notice how many times he refers to himself and takes credit for his blessings? Nebuchadnezzar wanted to be like God, lifting himself up. For his pride he would be humbled and exiled from his palace:

> He was driven away from people and ate grass like the ox. His body was drenched with the dew of heaven until his hair grew like the feathers of an eagle and his nails like the claws of a bird. (v. 33)

But thanks to God, he always offers a pathway of return and redemption.

> At the end of that time, I, Nebuchadnezzar, raised my eyes toward heaven, and my sanity was restored. Then I praised the Most High; I honored and glorified him who lives forever. (v. 34)

The great news is that Nebuchadnezzar humbled himself and was returned to his palace and restored. As we can be from our exile from God.

Here is the story of the prodigal son, one of the most popular and beloved of the stories told by Jesus. It, like the story of King Nebuchadnezzar, also depicts a joyous return from exile:

> There was a man who had two sons. The younger one said to his father, "Father, give me my share of the estate." So he divided his property between them.

> Not long after that, the younger son got together all he had, set off for a distant country and there squandered his wealth in wild living. After he had spent everything, there was a severe famine in that whole country, and he began to be in need. So he went and hired himself out to a citizen of that country, who sent him to his fields to feed pigs. He longed to fill his stomach with the pods that the pigs were eating, but no one gave him anything.

> When he came to his senses, he said, "How many of my father's hired servants have food to spare, and here I am starving to death! I will set out and go back to my father and say to him: Father, I have sinned against heaven and against you. I am no longer worthy to be called your son; make me like one of your hired servants." So he got up and went to his father.

> But while he was still a long way off, his father saw him and was filled with compassion for him; he ran to his son, threw his arms around him and kissed him.

> The son said to him, "Father, I have sinned against heaven and against you. I am no longer worthy to be called your son." But the father said to his servants, "Quick! Bring the best robe and put it on him. Put a ring on his finger and sandals on his feet. Bring the fattened calf and kill it. Let's have a feast and celebrate. For this son of mine was dead and is alive again; he was lost and is found." So they began to celebrate. (Luke 15:11–24)

The prodigal son's father graciously forgives him and restores him. And just as with the prodigal son, God reaches out to us in our exile, opens our eyes, and brings us to our senses.

Jesus made our return possible

God's plan for our journey and return and redemption did not come without a sacrifice.

His son, Jesus Christ, suffered and died for us to make it possible. When John the Baptist first saw Jesus, he turned to his disciples (John had disciples also, many of whom later followed Jesus) and said, "Look, the Lamb of God, who takes away the sin of the world!" (John 1:29).

Many other verses talk about how Jesus died for our sins, including:

> . . . that Christ died for our sins . . . (1 Corinthians 15:3)

> But God demonstrates his own love for us in this: While we were still sinners, Christ died for us. (Romans 5:8)

It was not an easy price to pay. 1 Peter 2:24 tells us, "He himself bore our sins in his body on the cross, so that we might die to sins and live for righteousness; by his wounds you have been healed."

In addition to dying for our sins and breaking the curse, in his loving kindness he has created a pathway to return to him. By his death and sacrifice, access to God is now open and available to us: "Through whom we have gained access by faith into this grace in which we now stand. And we boast in the hope of the glory of God" (Romans 5:2).

How should we respond?

God's desire is for us to always thank him for removing our sins and offering us forgiveness. We can rejoice and celebrate in our hearts and minds whenever we think of his sacrifice.

This is not a one-time thanks. We can live in a nearly continuous state of appreciation for his love sacrifice for us. This is what the Apostle Paul did at times:

> For I resolved to know nothing while I was with you except Jesus Christ and him crucified. (1 Corinthians 2:2)

Jesus demonstrated his great love by laying down his life for us. God wants us to know the great extent of this love sacrifice:

> I pray that you . . . may have power, together with all the Lord's holy people, to grasp how wide and long and high and deep is the love of Christ... (Ephesians 3:17, 18)

31

> No one has greater love than this: to lay down his
> life for his friends. (John 15:13)

We can know that his sacrifice and the laying down of his life extends far, far beyond the physical pain of the cross, as horrific as that was. We can also know that the depth and breadth of the sacrifice mirrors and is in proportion to the resulting blessing and benefit that we receive.

He was plotted against by his enemies with intent to harm (Matthew 26:3–4).
He protects us and ensures that no harm may come to us; he covers us with his blood and instructs his angels to guard us (2 Thessalonians 3:3, Exodus 12:13, Psalm 91:11).

He was betrayed by a close friend (Luke 22).
He is forever faithful to us. (Deuteronomy 7:9) He is for us, so who can be against us (Romans 8:31)?

He prayed in anguish in the garden, sweating drops of blood (Luke 22:44).
He comforts us in all our affliction (2 Corinthians 1:4).

He was surrounded by hatred and hostility (Psalm 69:4, Matthew 26:47–50).
He surrounds us with love and mercy and kindness (many verses, e.g. Psalm 103:4).

His friends (disciples) fled and deserted him (Matthew 26:56).
He is with us and will never forsake us (Deuteronomy 31:6).

He was held captive and in bondage (Matthew 26:50).

He releases and liberates us and sets us free from all that entangles us and encumbers us and holds us in chains (Galatians 5:1, Hebrews 12:1–3).

He was led by his enemies who intended to destroy him (Matthew 26:57).
He leads us in his glorious paths (Psalm 23:3, 2 Corinthians 2:14).

He was falsely accused and no one, not even himself, spoke in his defense (Matthew 27:12).
He intercedes and advocates for us and defends us (Romans 8:34, Psalm 121:7–8).

He was innocent, and yet condemned (Matthew 27:22–24).
We are guilty, and yet pardoned (Romans 3:28).

He was horribly whipped (John 19:1).
By his wounds we are healed (Isaiah 53:5, 1 Peter 2:24).

He was filthy and dirty (inferred from his treatment).
He purifies us and cleanses us from all unrighteousness (1 John 1:7, 9).

He was publicly stripped, humiliated, and disgraced (Matthew 27:28).
He covers us and dresses us in his white robes of righteousness, his clean linens, his shining garments (Isaiah 61:10, Revelation 19:8).

He was terribly disfigured (Isaiah 52:14).
He makes us beautiful (Ecclesiastes 3:11).

He was forced to carry his cross, the sin of the world (John 19:17, Isaiah 53:12).

He lifts off and bears our burdens and infirmities and problems and afflictions (Psalm 68:19, Matthew 11:28).

He was weak and stumbled and fell while carrying the cross (tradition). His strength is made perfect in our weakness (2 Corinthians 12:9). We can do all things through Christ who strengthens us (Philippians 4:13); we run and do not grow weary, walk and do not grow faint (Isaiah 40:31).

He was nailed to a cross. His body was broken and his blood poured out (Matthew 26:26-28).
He was pierced for our transgressions and crushed for our sins. He took upon himself the punishment that brings us peace (Matthew 26:26–28, Isaiah 53:5). He who knew no sin became sin for us so that we can become the righteousness of God (2 Corinthians 5:21).

He was thirsty and was given vinegar to drink (John 19:28–30). He gives us living waters to drink that well up unto eternal life (John 4:14).

He could not breath, he was asphyxiated (the nature of crucifixion). He breathes his Spirit into us (John 20:22).

He died as he gave up his spirit (Matthew 27:50).
He raises us to new life by his Spirit (Romans 8:11).

He was cast down into darkness (Ephesians 4:8 and the Apostles Creed).
He lifts us up and seats us with him in the heavenlies, and his face shines on us (Ephesians 2:6, Numbers 6:24–26).

Practice: On good days I pray through and contemplate the sacrifice of Christ. I have found that it has strengthened my faith and helped me to be more appreciative.

Chapter 5

The Good Shepherd Waits and Searches for Us

While we have been astray, busy living our lives in our outer being, God has been opening a way for our journey, as we saw from the last chapter. But our return to him is not automatic. Because we acquired the knowledge of good and evil, now we are responsible for choosing to come to him and make the journey with him. Only he cares enough and has the power to bring us to himself. We cannot do it on our own.

Who is the Shepherd?

Psalm 23:1 says, "The Lord is my shepherd." More specifically, Jesus is our Shepherd, the Good Shepherd. Jesus referred to himself as exactly that. (John 10:11)

He is our Good Shepherd who leads us:

> I am the good shepherd. (John 10:11)

And he was referring to himself when he said:

> The one who enters by the gate is the shepherd of
> the sheep. (John 10:2)

From all of this we can recognize that the Good Shepherd is the
only one that can lead us on our spiritual journey. It is God's
design.

The Good Shepherd beckons to us

Jesus, the Good Shepherd, says "Come, follow me". (Matthew
4:19) His arms are spread wide. His heart is even wider. He
promises:

> "Come to me, all you who are weary and burdened,
> and I will give you rest. (Matthew 11:28)
>
> "I am the light of the world. Whoever follows me
> will never walk in darkness, but will have the light
> of life." (John 8:12)

Undoing the curse – proclaiming we need him

Sheep, whether they realize it or not, need a shepherd.

Recall how in the garden humanity wanted to be like God. Indeed,
this is how we were tricked and deceived. For the enemy said, "For
God knows that when you eat from it your eyes will be opened,
and you will be like God, knowing good and evil" (Genesis 3:5).

We did not wait for God to lead us or guide us. Instead, we listened
to the leading of the enemy of our souls. By taking action without

God and trying to become like him, we proclaimed that we did not need God to lead and guide us.

Thanks to God, though, now we are given the opportunity to undo this aspect of the curse. How? By admitting our need for God. By acknowledging that we are completely and entirely dependent on him, on the Good Shepherd, Jesus. By proclaiming that we want to follow him—him and only him.

The Good Shepherd finds us when we are lost

Deciding to follow Jesus, our Good Shepherd, seems fairly simple and easy. But for many of us it is not. Why?

Some of us may not feel worthy. No matter how many times we have heard "God loves you just the way you are" or "come as you are," we are so deeply programmed to feel we are not good enough for someone to love us and care about us or for something really good to happen to us.

Or we may not feel that we can trust anyone to lead us and guide us and rule over us. Perhaps because we were betrayed or violated by loved ones.

Or perhaps because we feel strong and independent and prefer to be the captain of our fate.

For any of these or other reasons, we find that we cannot or do not know how to come and give ourselves to the Good Shepherd. We are encumbered by deep programming that keeps us from it. We have bought the lies of the enemy of our souls, even if we do not realize it.

This is the state of being of one of the lost sheep that Jesus talks about—the one that has not only wandered but cannot seem to return when it is called by the Good Shepherd.

Being a lost sheep sounds really bad. Being lost is bad, and being a sheep is bad. One seems to imply deficiency; the other seems to imply weakness. Fortunately, we have this wrong.

Heaven, and our Good Shepherd, love those who cannot seem to easily return to him. The Good Shepherd not only loves them, but he ventures out and searches for and finds them:

> What do you think? If a man owns a hundred sheep, and one of them wanders away, will he not leave the ninety-nine on the hills and go to look for the one that wandered off? And if he finds it, truly I tell you, he is happier about that one sheep than about the ninety-nine that did not wander off. (Matthew 18:12–13)

If the lost sheep is the one that gets the help and attention and love from the Good Shepherd, then we should want to be the lost sheep. Thanks to God, with the right attitude, we can each be a lost sheep.

It is not about being somehow wrong or flawed or weak. Rather, it is about knowing how much we need his help. We must just become aware of this fact and admit it. In fact, let us not admit it hesitantly. Everyone starts off lost and far away from God. Let us instead rejoice and be thankful for this.

We can tell Jesus, "We need you for every breath. For every moment to exist and think and move. And to become one with you for eternity. We can only be fulfilled in you." "For in him we live and move and have our being" (Acts 17:28).

> *He tends his flock like a shepherd:*
> *He gathers the lambs in his arms*
> *and carries them close to his heart;*
> *he gently leads those that have young.*
> —Isaiah 40:11

We must also saturate ourselves with the truth that Jesus wants to come to us, find us, and rescue us and bring us back to him. This is not something he finds unpleasant or drudgery. It is what he wants to do. He desires to do it. He is designed to do it. It is a manifestation, an exercise, of his great love and compassion and mercy.

Practice: Envision Christ as looking down upon us individually. Feel how his eyes and attention are upon us in love and kindness and compassion. Every moment. Regardless and independently of our thoughts, our words, and our actions.

Prayer: Dear Lord, we are always wandering. Help us to know it and realize it and rejoice that you search and find us. Help us to take a moment to cast ourselves upon you and sink back into you in our minds and hearts and souls—our inner being.

What if we still find it difficult to believe?

Maybe our minds still resist the idea that there is a God out there and that he wants to change and transform us through a spiritual journey to experience complete fulfillment in divine love with Christ.

This is okay too, because if even one small corner of our heart or mind hopes and desires that it is true and wants it, this is enough for our Good Shepherd to work. It is the seed in our soul. Just give the Good Shepherd this tiny speck that wants him and ask him to rescue and heal and grow and transform. Each day we can go with this small speck of our being and present it to him. He is faithful.

> *"I do believe; help me overcome my unbelief!"*
> —Mark 9:24

He seeks out the lost sheep

Our good shepherd is not the sort of leader or guide who simply broadcasts instructions or information about what way to go. He is not just the conductor of music or the coach on the field. He does show us the way on our journey, but he does much more than this.

He first and foremost finds us where we are and connects with us. He knows us and even feels with us exactly how we feel and what we are going through. That is what he means by seeking and finding us.

Our mistake is often that we think we must meet him where we think he is, in his greatness and his glory. But instead he finds us and meets us where he is like us. He is most like us in his sacrifice, because this is where he rescues us—in our lostness and weakness and emptiness and sin and exile:

> And so Jesus also suffered outside the city gate to make the people holy through his own blood. Let us, then, go to him outside the camp, bearing the disgrace he bore. (Hebrews 13:12–13)

He will later take us to strength and victory and glory.

He is there in every weakness and failure and sin. He knows and feels what we know and feel. He is a God of empathy and compassion. He feels it as we do in every situation.

How do we know this? In him every good thing exists and has from before time began, since something cannot be created unless it is first in the mind of the designer and creator. And now, since he died on the cross, he understands and feels everything. Not in the sense that he has sinned, but in all of the fallout, all of the guilt and shame, all of the regret, all of the disappointment. We will explore more on this in later chapters.

> *God made him who had no sin to be sin for us, so that*
> *in him we might become the righteousness of God.*
> —2 Corinthians 5:21

> *He himself bore our sins in his body on the cross, so*
> *that we might die to sins and live for righteousness;*
> *by his wounds you have been healed.*
> —1 Peter 2:24

We can be like the man Jesus spoke about who stood humbly in the temple and admitted his insufficiency. The one who beat his chest and cried out, "God, have mercy on me, a sinner!" (Luke 18:13).

Our flaws and weaknesses are there not to make us feel bad about ourselves, cause us to hide and pretend they don't exist, or overcome us. Rather, they exist to remind us of how much we need God.

It is natural to want to overcome or escape the feeling of weakness and insufficiency and neediness. But now we are set free to appreciate and welcome and embrace our weaknesses! Since our failures and weaknesses are real and exist regardless of whether we admit to them or not, now God turns them to good. It is a good place to be.

Prayer: Thank you, God, for our weaknesses. They remind us of our need for you. Our sense of need for you can become a real and powerful force in our inner being.

Practice: Think of what is bothering you and concerning you today. Now envision, understand, and believe that God is there with you in this exact situation and condition, in your thoughts and feelings. You just now need to recognize and accept him in this and allow him to lead you in it and through it while holding your hand.

Deciding whether to follow the Good Shepherd

The Good Shepherd finds us, and then he invites us and calls us to follow him on our spiritual journey, all the way. This is an all-or-nothing deal.

We must from this point decide and determine that we are willing to give up everything, pay any price, to be one with Christ. No matter what happens. No matter how we feel. We must consider the cost, otherwise we are sure to give up:

> And whoever does not carry their cross and follow me cannot be my disciple. Suppose one of you wants to build a tower. Won't you first sit down and estimate the cost to see if you have enough money to complete it? For if you lay the foundation

and are not able to finish it, everyone who sees it will ridicule you, saying, "This person began to build and wasn't able to finish." (Luke 14:27–30)

Again, the kingdom of heaven is like a merchant looking for fine pearls. When he found one of great value, he went away and sold everything he had and bought it. (Matthew 13:45–46)

It is said beautifully in the song "Christ is Enough" by Hillsong Worship:

I have decided to follow Jesus
No turning back
No turning back
The cross before me
The world behind me
No turning back
No turning back

God has revealed to us the best key to being sure we will press forward and not turn back. It is that we can continuously remind ourselves that with Christ we have all to gain that is of true value and nothing to lose of any lasting value.

This is beautifully illustrated in how many of the crowd following Jesus deserted him because he offered a "hard teaching." Jesus turned and confronted those who remained, asking them, "You do not want to leave too, do you?" And Peter answered, "Lord, to whom shall we go? You have the words of eternal life" (John 6:67, 68).

We can also encourage ourselves with this—that we should "press on toward the goal to win the prize for which God has called [us] heavenward in Christ Jesus" (Philippians 3:14).

Contemplate: Are we ready to make this decision? Are we at peace with paying any price to gain oneness with Christ?

> *I consider everything a loss because of the*
> *surpassing worth of knowing Christ Jesus my*
> *Lord, for whose sake I have lost all things.*
> —Philippians 3:8

What if we were to look back?

What if we decide to return to our old life? It is a very terrible thing indeed. Consider the outcomes for Lot's wife in Genesis 19. Lot was Abraham's nephew. He and his wife and family were dwelling in Sodom, a city on the plains of Jordan with much wealth but also much evil. God sent two angels down to rescue and deliver Lot and his family before God would destroy the city.

The angels warned them, "Flee for your lives! Don't look back, and don't stop . . ." (Genesis 19:17). Lot's wife, however, did look back, "and she became a pillar of salt" (v. 26). A very high price to pay.

Or we have the case of the Israelites in the desert who wished to return to Egypt. The Israelites were living as slaves in Egypt when God sent his servant Moses to deliver them. God granted them favor by bringing them out of Egypt and helping them escape the Egyptian army. They had to pass through the wilderness on the way to Israel, the Promised Land. The desert was difficult, even though God fully provided for their needs.

Some wanted to rebel and return to Egypt. In Numbers 16, some of them even said to Moses, "Isn't it enough that you have brought us up out of a land flowing with milk and honey [Egypt] to kill us in the wilderness? And now you also want to lord it over us!" (v. 13).

Can you imagine how they could have called the land of slavery and oppression "a land flowing with milk and honey"? How insulting to God and Moses, since God had promised to lead them to the Promised Land (Israel) that he described as flowing with milk and honey. They had turned it upside down.

Moses called all of those who wanted to rebel to present themselves in front of their tents, before God. Here is what happened to those who wanted to rebel and return to Egypt:

> Now it came to pass, as he [Moses] finished speaking all these words, that the ground split apart under them, and the earth opened its mouth and swallowed them up, with their households and all the men with Korah, with all their goods. So they and all those with them went down alive into the pit; the earth closed over them, and they perished from among the assembly. (Numbers 16:31–32)

Finally, here is a very strongly worded warning from Scripture:

> If they have escaped the corruption of the world by knowing our Lord and Savior Jesus Christ and are again entangled in it and are overcome, they are worse off at the end than they were at the beginning. (2 Peter 2:20)

The solution

In the garden we made a decision based on perceived benefits. The fruit looked pleasant, and we thought it would taste good and give us the knowledge of good and evil so that we would be like God. We became slaves instead.

Now we can make the decision to pursue Christ on the journey, not based on perceived benefits along the way but out of obedience to the Good Shepherd. In choosing to become true followers of Christ, we thought we were losing our freedom, but really we are finally gaining true freedom. True spiritual freedom is not the opportunity to make choices but rather the power to become one with Christ, as we were designed to do.

> *. . do not use your freedom as a cover-up*
> *for evil; live as God's slaves..*
> —1 Peter 2:16

Chapter 6

Becoming Followers of the Good Shepherd

To gain insight into how we can learn to truly and faithfully follow the Good Shepherd, we once again return to the garden before sin. We stood before God like this:

> Adam and his wife were both naked, and they felt no shame. (Genesis 2:25)

This is much more than simply a statement regarding physical condition. It shows how humanity started in a state of innocence, without self-consciousness, without judgment, without the need for hiding anything, without the need for money or possessions, without a care for reputation and stature or power or control or safety.

But then sin entered the picture, causing us to hide from God:

> Then the man and his wife heard the sound of the Lord God as he was walking in the garden in the cool of the day, and they hid from the Lord God among the trees of the garden. (Genesis 3:8)

As we explored Chapter 2, "Separation from God," the knowledge of good and evil has sucked us into a never-ending struggle of seeing and knowing our sin and faults and shortcomings, and responding by attempting to cover ourselves. The only thing this achieves is to separate us from God.

Thanks to God we can now undo this part of the curse. We can present ourselves before him as often as possible, at least a few times each day.

Practice: Here is one way that I like. Stand (or any position will do) with face upturned, hands either in the conventional praying position with palms facing one another or across the chest, palms facing the heart. Breathe deeply to help clear the mind—long inhales in through the nose, slow exhales through the mouth. Be silent and still the mind for a moment and know he is God (Psalm 46:10). Then know that you are in God's presence, in your inner being. Naked and unashamed. Empty-handed, with no agenda. Cast off even your successes and accomplishments and titles (Revelation 4:10). Offer your body up to him as a living sacrifice (Romans 12:1).

You can then gently proclaim and tell God, "I am yours and you are mine" (Song of Solomon 2:16), "I am your property and possession" (Numbers 18:20), and "You bought me for a price" (1 Corinthians 6:20).

Now know that whatever condition you find yourself in, the Good Shepherd loves you and accepts you!

The greatest happiness of life is the conviction that we are loved;
loved for ourselves, or rather, loved in spite of ourselves.
—Victor Hugo

Be silent and open before him

Our souls grow through the opening of a channel between God and our inner being. This is why we practice being still and directing our attention on him and presenting ourselves to him and laying ourselves, all our thoughts and feelings, open and surrendered to him. It is why in Psalm 46:10 God says, "Be still, and know that I am God."

This is a sustained silence. We should focus our minds on his greatness and holiness. He is perfect and without movement or change. He is "one God and Father of all, who is over all and through all and in all" (Ephesians 4:6).

Fixing our attention on the Good Shepherd

We should have our Good Shepherd in mind, cultivate being in his presence and attentive and focused on him through all of our daily activities. We can rest in him in our inner being as we perform our activities and go about our business in our outer being:

> Set your minds on things above, not on earthly things. (Colossians 3:2)

> And we all, who with unveiled faces contemplate the Lord's glory, are being transformed into his image with ever-increasing glory, which comes from the Lord, who is the Spirit. (2 Corinthians 3:18)

> . . . fixing our eyes on Jesus, the pioneer and perfecter of faith. (Hebrews 12:2)

I keep my eyes always on the Lord. (Psalm 16:8)

There are many ways to help make this happen. One approach is the ancient practice of thresholds. Before starting any particular activity, we can turn our attention upwards to Jesus, commit our time and activity to him, and ask him to be with us and lead us and live through us in this activity. We can dedicate each activity and moment to him and ask that it would be done in his strength, his will, and his love and for his purposes:

> Commit your way to the Lord; trust in him and he will do this: He will make your righteous reward shine like the dawn, your vindication like the noonday sun. (Psalm 37:5–6)

At the end of the activity we can again set aside a moment, silence our mind and body, turn our attention to him, and give him thanks. If we are not happy with how things are going, we can remember that his ways and understanding are far above our own, so we shall withhold judgment and instead believe by faith that he is working our situation out for good and therefore we can rejoice in it:

> And we know that in all things God works for the good of those who love him, who have been called according to his purpose. (Romans 8:28)

Practice: You may find that awareness of God and focusing on him are easiest at night. I have found that as the cares of the day fade I can more effectively connect with Christ and gaze up to him. Take full advantage of whatever times and places work best for you.

Call on his name

We can receive power by calling on God's name. When we call on his name, we are really asking him to come into the moments of our lives to empower us and guide us and flow through us.

Not just in times of need or desperation. Anytime. Not just to ask for help, but rather to open and strengthen our connection with him. We tell him how much we love him and need him, how much we need him to build into our inner life so we may feel his presence.

> *In my distress I called to the Lord, and he answered me.*
> —Jonah 2:2

The following story from *The Little Flowers of St. Francis of Assisi* demonstrates perfectly how calling on God is more than a brief and casual act:

> The first companion of St Francis was Brother Bernard of Assisi, who was converted in the following way: St Francis had not yet taken the religious habit, though he had renounced the world, and had so given himself to penance and mortification that many looked upon him as one out of his mind. He was scoffed at as a madman, was rejected and despised by his relations and by strangers, who threw stones and mud at him when he passed; yet he went on his way, accepting these insults as patiently as if he had been deaf and dumb. Then Bernard of Assisi, one of the richest and most learned nobles of the city, began to consider deeply the conduct of St Francis; how utterly he despised the world, how patiently he suffered injuries, and

how his faith remained firm, though he had been for two years an object of contempt and rejected by all. He began to think and say within himself, "It is evident that this brother must have received great graces from God"; and so resolved to invite him to sup and to sleep in his house. St Francis having accepted the invitation, Bernard, who was resolved to contemplate the sanctity of his guest, ordered a bed to be prepared for him in his own room, where a lamp burned all night. Now St Francis, in order to conceal his sanctity, so soon as he entered the room, threw himself upon the bed, pretending to fall asleep. Bernard likewise soon after went to bed, and began to snore as if sleeping soundly. On this, St Francis, thinking that Bernard was really fast asleep, got up and began to pray. Raising his hands and eyes to heaven, he exclaimed with great devotion and fervour, "My God! my God!" at the same time weeping bitterly; and thus he remained on his knees all night, repeating with great love and fervour the words, "My God! my God!" and none others.

And this he did because, being enlightened by the Holy Spirit, he contemplated and admired the divine majesty of God, who deigned to take pity on the perishing world, and to save not only the soul of Francis, his poor little one, but those of many others also through his means.

. . .

Then Bernard, seeing by the light of the lamp the devout actions of St Francis and the expression of his countenance, and devoutly considering the words he uttered, was touched by the Holy Spirit, and resolved to change his life.[5]

We might likewise call on his name, even while offering up ourselves to him in surrender and devotion.

He is our identity

When we identify with someone (or something) very closely, it is almost as if we become a part of them and they become a part of us. It can be very powerful. Powerful for good or bad, depending on who or what we identify with.

We can constantly remind ourselves that we are attached to God in our heart and soul. He is the greatest part of us. We are more and more his reflection.

We can begin to think of him not as a separate person but as someone we are a part of. We feel as he feels, think as he thinks, do as he does. It is God's will that we identify with Christ in a very tight and close and powerful manner:

> I am the vine; you are the branches. If you remain in me and I in you, you will bear much fruit; apart from me you can do nothing. (John 15:5)

> Whom have I in heaven but you?
> And earth has nothing I desire besides you.
> (Psalm 73:25)

---

[5] https://www.ccel.org/ccel/ugolino/flowers.html

Phase Two: Providing for Us

Our Shepherd knows what we need, and what we do not need, for our journey. We can joyfully receive his provision, give thanks, and experience contentment. He feeds us with his Word. He strengthens us. He provides his Spirit. This is where the Psalmist says, "I lack nothing. He makes me lie down in green pastures, he leads me beside quiet waters, he refreshes my soul" (Psalm 23:1–3).

In Christ we find all that we need. He alone is sufficient. In him are all things:

> The Son is the image of the invisible God, the firstborn over all creation. For in him all things were created: things in heaven and on earth, visible and invisible, whether thrones or powers or rulers or authorities; all things have been created through him and for him. He is before all things, and in him all things hold together. And he is the head of the body, the church; he is the beginning and the firstborn from among the dead, so that in everything he might have the supremacy. For God was pleased to have all his fullness dwell in him, and through him to reconcile to himself all things . . . (Colossians 1:15–20)

We have been deceived into wanting and desiring many things. God will now show us that we need not concern ourselves with these things that will not truly satisfy us. He will lead us into perfect contentment.

Chapter 7

Preparing for the Journey

Once we establish that Jesus is our Good Shepherd and we are his followers, we need to prepare for the journey. There are some things that God wants us to know and believe that will strengthen us and edify us. These things will shape our mindset, our expectations, and our mental resolve, which early on can make such a huge difference.

Make the journey our primary purpose

"For a small reward, a man will hurry away on a long journey; while for eternal life, many will hardly take a single step."
— Thomas à Kempis

Many of us have established our own personal goals, missions, and purposes. Perhaps they have to do with education and career, relationships, sports or music, vacations, or hobbies. Or maybe as life moves on we create our bucket list of things we want to do before it is too late. We may have read books and articles on mission and purpose and success and effectiveness. *Seven Habits.*

Purpose Driven Life. Many others. These can be very good and beneficial.

So now will our spiritual journey in Christ become one additional goal, purpose, or mission? Something that competes with other equally important priorities? Or should it be much more? Something that lies outside and above all other purposes and goals and missions?

To meet with success, our journey to oneness with Christ must be a supra purpose. God wills that it be far above every other purpose as the heavens are above the earth, beyond every other goal as eternity lies beyond the limited duration of this life.

Jesus made this clear when he said, "Whoever wants to be my disciple must deny themselves and take up their cross and follow me. For whoever wants to save their life will lose it, but whoever loses their life for me will find it." (Matthew 16:24–26). And the Apostle Paul also alluded to this when he said, "Do you not know that in a race all the runners run, but only one gets the prize? Run in such a way as to get the prize" (1 Corinthians 9:24).

How does this work? Our journey is not something that we can pursue with some of our time. Or with some of our energy. Rather it shall be a continuous pursuit and conscious awareness—a script running behind all of our other scripts.

Think of the many causes humans have given their all to achieve. Things that fade and disappear. Unlike these, our spiritual journey is worth every ounce of ourselves. It is our grand purpose and design.

We can decide now to dedicate our lives to this one great calling— our spiritual journey.

Believe that the inner life is to be our real life

We need to acquire the mindset and believe by faith that we have a beautiful and powerful inner life that God is creating in us, one that is ultimately infinite and eternal. This grand truth needs to sink deep into our psyche. We must know it and believe it and continuously hope and dwell in it. It should encourage us in our up moments and comfort us in our down moments.

Spiritual realities are very real and powerful and will transform us in ways that physical and mental activities can never accomplish. Our spiritual journey can take us to places that we can't travel to in the physical world or comprehend in our human thinking and reasoning.

Our minds and hearts and souls are transformable! We must believe this.

Even if we agree, we may find this truth to be difficult to really believe deep down inside. This is because we have been deceived and programmed into believing that the outer world—the material world along with our circumstances and environment and what we call life—is the only truly real existence. It is always before our eyes, demanding our constant attention.

To overcome, we must step forward in faith and continuously remind ourselves of our true home:

> But our citizenship is in heaven. And we eagerly await a Savior from there, the Lord Jesus Christ. (Philippians 3:20)

Adopt the right view of the purpose of this life

How shall we then view our life in the outer world? All the things and circumstances and busy affairs of life?

We need to remind ourselves that the true purpose of our outer being is to feed and build our souls. Like rain and sunshine on the fields. The idea is that the temporary should grow and sustain what is permanent.

> *The world's thy ship and not thy home.*
> —Thérèse de Lisieux

In the Garden we made a decision to use a mere thing, a piece of fruit hanging on a tree, for our self-interest and self-promotion. Thereby we created a pattern of looking to temporary things in this way.

But now we can see that we have the opportunity to begin undoing the curse by asking God to use each object and each circumstance for his purpose in our life. God can use them, those that seem good and those that seem bad, to advance us on our journey. As a result, we can begin viewing them as friends and helpers.

We need to recognize that all material possessions, all circumstances, and all of the busy affairs of our lives here are of no importance in and of themselves. They only have value as God breathes into them so that they might serve his purpose.

We primarily grow, or have the opportunity to grow, by struggles in this life. Not by good times, successes, or ease. Understanding this, we can develop an entirely different view of our problems and challenges. Give thanks and praise in and through all things.

We can also loosen and lighten up since now in Christ we can see life as helping and supporting our inner journey. We are free to view our life as an adventure. We can believe by faith that all things are working to advance us on our journey (Romans 8:28). It is all in how we see and respond to our circumstances, to all that happens to us.

Don't give up

> *In what torn ship soever I embark,*
> *That ship shall be my emblem of thy Ark*
> —John Donne, "A Hymn to Christ"

The spiritual journey to oneness with Christ is long and difficult. Why is it important that we recognize this? Because we must view it from that perspective so that we continue to seek and pursue and do not give up or look for the exit when the going gets tough:

> For which of you, intending to build a tower, does
> not sit down first and count the cost, whether he
> has enough to finish it— (Luke 14:28)

The spiritual journey requires the greatest patience, perseverance, and endurance of all.

We learn early on in life that some things, like receiving an education, making money, training for a sport, or learning an art form, require a great amount of investment and time and focus and sweat equity. We also learn that they are worth the investment.

Now, is this true of how we regard spiritual growth? Perhaps many of us have not anticipated much personal sacrifice and hard work. Perhaps Christianity, faith, and the spiritual life have been presented to us with an emphasis on their many benefits. But like with anything, the benefits come with a cost.

Sometimes what we expect from our faith falls short and we find ourselves disappointed. We can be tempted to give up. We can feel that results are taking too long to come to fruition and are not worth the cost, the sacrifices, the risks, and the difficulties.

If we stop and consider the reasons for wanting to give up, we may realize that they relate to the self. It is that *I* am not getting what *I* had hoped for.

Here is the real thing: we cannot view our spiritual journey in terms of anticipated benefits. We cannot fully know now the magnitude of the wonders of becoming one with Christ. Our goal is not for our present self. It must be for Christ. Being one with Christ means that all we do for him, we will then share with him—all things and treasures and eternity with Christ.

> *I served the Lord with great humility and with*
> *tears and in the midst of severe testing . . .*
> —Acts 20:19

Why else might we bail out from our journey? Maybe because we are not sure how to proceed. We stand at the crossroads and do not know the direction, so we turn around and go back.

If we genuinely seek God for his will, his truth, and his path, we can trust that he will provide. We must believe by faith he will show us the way. If he appears not to, then we will believe that our very pondering and seeking and asking is his pathway. We are on the path whether we think so or not. Hopefully, ideas shared by others, including those here in this book, will be helpful.

A great insight is revealed in *The Velveteen Rabbit*, or *How Toys Become Real*, by Margery Williams. It is a spiritual classic disguised as a cute children's story. When the main character, the stuffed rabbit, asks the old, wise hobby horse how one becomes real, he answers:

> It doesn't happen all at once. You become. It takes a long time. That's why it doesn't happen often to people who break easily, or have sharp edges, or who have to be carefully kept. Generally, by the time you are Real, most of your hair has been loved off, and your eyes drop out and you get loose in the joints and very shabby. But these things don't matter at all, because once you are Real you can't be ugly, except to people who don't understand.

How much do we want it? Time will be the test. Will we be resolved to continue, even if . . .

- we see no visible progress and it seems fruitless, without any real payoff?
- we grow bored and tired of it?
- no one understands or cares about our journey and our efforts?

Understand that things work differently in the inner being

When our kids were growing up they would sometimes declare that it was "opposite day." Then all rules and conditions were to be the opposite of normal. This, of course, allowed them a new freedom to break old rules!

With God in our inner being, many things are opposite from how they work in the outer being. We must be aware of this to experience success. Here are a few examples:

- We are weak, that his strength may be made perfect. (2 Corinthians 12:9)
- We are empty, that he might fill us with his fullness. (Ephesians 3:19)
- We are blind, that he may give us true vision. (Isaiah 42:7)
- We are in darkness, that he might rescue us and bring us into the light. (Colossians 1:13)
- We have and are nothing, that he might share his everything with us. (2 Corinthians 8:9)
- We lower ourselves so that he might lift us up. (James 4:10)
- We know nothing and become fools so he might share his wisdom with us. (1 Corinthians 3:18)
- We experience sorrow and grieving for a season so that his joy may overflow in us. (Psalm 30:11)
- We confess our failure and shortcomings and sins so that their power to harm us is removed and we are forgiven. (James 5:16)

Chapter 8

I Shall Not Be in Want

Have you ever started a trip when you were lacking something important? It may be you were hungry or thirsty, or tired and without sleep, or without needed supplies and provisions. You just knew that things would not go well. Thankfully, for our spiritual journey, God has us covered.

God promises that we shall not be in want: "The LORD is my shepherd; I shall not want" (Psalm 23:1 ESV). He includes it in the very beginning of the chapter for this very reason; he knows we need the reassurance that we will not lack what we need for the journey.

This seems to be a very large promise indeed. When we stop and spend time considering our thoughts and feelings, are we not a bundle of desires? We want our physical needs to be met, we want fulfilling relationships, we want safety and security, we want social significance and success, we want to feel that we're making an impact, and we want to feel good about ourselves. Let's look at how our wants come into play, and what it means that God will provide for us along the way.

The origin of our wants

As with so many of our struggles, we must go back to the garden to gain understanding. Humanity ate from the tree of the knowledge of good and evil because it was "good for food and pleasing to the eye, and also desirable for gaining wisdom" (Genesis 3:6). Though we had all of our real needs met, we were not satisfied. We wanted more pleasure, and we wanted more wisdom.

This brought a dire consequence:

> To Adam he [God] said, ". . . Cursed is the ground because of you; through painful toil you will eat food from it all the days of your life. It will produce thorns and thistles for you, and you will eat the plants of the field." (Genesis 3:17–18)

Notice how we have gone from eating plentiful fruit hanging from the trees in the garden to eating plants of the field. The fruit on the trees was elevated and easy to pick and eat. Now we are stooped down to the dirt, struggling to meet our needs.

Most importantly for our spiritual journey, this created a new pattern of wanting and desiring and craving, even for things what we really do not need. Material possessions. Success. Popularity. Pleasure. Excitement. Prominence. Attention. Compliments. Achievements. On and on. We have created and generated for ourselves discontentment and the constant need for more and better.

While what it is that we desire differs from person to person, the condition of wanting is always there in one form or another. Our lives are consumed by this endless pursuit. Sadly, not only does it take up our time and energy, but it also breeds dissatisfaction, frustration, anger, jealousy, covetousness, insecurity. All the things that keep our souls empty.

The deceitfulness of our wants

Because of our programming to strive for and focus on what we want, we do not always see the blessings of God. We prefer the temporary and fading things on the ground rather than what is elevated.

We need to remember that God instructs us to "fix our eyes not on what is seen, but on what is unseen, since what is seen is temporary, but what is unseen is eternal" (2 Corinthians 4:18). Remember that "each person is tempted when they are dragged away by their own evil desire and enticed" (James 1:14).

We can see how the constant demand of these desires and compulsions and wants and urges are obstructing us from experiencing spiritual growth, as well as stealing our peace and joy.

These wants and desires may be deeply wired into us. They may have been passed down from generation to generation. We may have given them a deep hold on us.

We are deceived into thinking that if and when we get what we want we will then have peace, security, success, and value. Unfortunately, desire is insatiable. When we acquire something, or meet a goal, or satisfy a craving, we typically experience a short sense of relief, followed by more desiring and compulsion and craving and longing.

Thankfully, there are some actions we can take to overcome deceitful and counterproductive desires.

Looking under the hood

To unmask the deceit, we should look under the hood at each of our wants. We should ask God for revelation and insight into them. Each time we feel a need or desire or discontentment or unhappiness, we can ask ourselves, what is the source or cause of it? Is it truly some need, or is it simply in our heads?

If it is not a true need, we can ask God for deliverance from the desire, the attachment. He can alleviate and eliminate these false desires. He may do it by revealing the truth about our desires and how they are distortions of our true needs that are to be satisfied in Christ. When he does this for you, "you will know the truth, and the truth will set you free" (John 8:32).

Practice: Looking at how my mind works and the script of my thoughts, I realize that most of my discretionary thoughts really boil down to wanting to feel better about myself. I feel socially awkward, so I review previous interactions and think of ways to be "cooler." I want to feel smart, so I think of ways to impress with my knowledge and brains. I feel insecure in relationships, so I think of ways to make things seem better and work more smoothly and to get more compliments. I compare myself with others. I fret and wonder if I can meet the expectations I have placed on myself and others have placed on me.

For all of these thoughts that keep dominating me, I realize that all are satisfied in Christ. I can connect my mind with him and cultivate a sense of satisfaction and sufficiency and completeness.

I was just driving home this morning from an event. As I was driving, I felt a vague sense of dissatisfaction, insecurity, and failure concerning how it went. Then I decided to instead just attach my mind to Jesus and have him with me and envisioned him handling all things. He was even handling how I flowed in traffic. It was wonderful. He set me at ease. I was comfortable and content in him as we took every turn and stopped and started at every traffic light together.

And God is able to bless you abundantly, so that
in all things at all times, having all that you
need, you will abound in every good work.
—2 Corinthians 9:8

Speak the truth

1 John 2:17 says, "The world and its desires pass away, but whoever does the will of God lives forever." This and other verses like it remind us that what we want in this life, in our outer being, is temporary and passing away. We should speak this truth into every situation of want.

God has something much better in store for us. He will deliver us from whatever situation we find ourselves in. Our outer beings will be what they are. Our lives may blow in the wind and tempest, but we have an inner space to be safe and grow with God. A rock to dwell on. Let the winds and waves do their thing, we shall be ok with it:

> "Therefore everyone who hears these words of mine and puts them into practice is like a wise man who built his house on the rock. 25 The rain came down, the streams rose, and the winds blew and beat against that house; yet it did not fall, because it had its foundation on the rock.".
> (Matthew 7:24–25 ESV)

We can remind ourselves of the truth– our wants and desires are programmed in our minds. We can know they are foreign to our souls and true existence. Programming takes time to change, but it is possible. We will explore more on this in later chapters.

God is sufficient

We should contemplate on the truth that God is sufficient for us:

> And my God will supply every need of yours according to his riches in glory in Christ Jesus. (Philippians 4:19)
>
> My grace is sufficient for you, for my power is made perfect in weakness. (2 Corinthians 12:9)
>
> Whom have I in heaven but you?
>   And earth has nothing I desire besides you.
> My flesh and my heart may fail,
>   but God is the strength of my heart
>   and my portion forever. (Psalm 73:25–26)

Dissatisfaction, frustration, anger, jealousy—all flow from a sense of deficiency.

Practice: Cultivate a sense of sufficiency, fulfillment, adequacy, and contentment. God is more than enough for our souls, our inner beings. He is handling everything. And he is ready to share all this generously and lavishly. We can speak words of sufficiency and contentment. We can proclaim that God is providing all that we need for the life and pathway he has for us:

But godliness with contentment is great gain. For we brought nothing into the world, and we can take nothing out of it. But if we have food and clothing, we will be content with that. (1 Timothy 6:6–8)

We can be positive and know that all is good in Christ. We can cultivate a lightness of being as we float through this life. Every situation is good if we invite Christ into it.

> *. . . love works so in me*
> *that whether things go well or badly*
> *love turns them to one sweetness*
> *transforming the soul in itself.*
> —St. John of the Cross, A Gloss

Be thankful

It is the old truism—we will be far more content when we see the glass as half full, not half empty. We can appreciate and give thanks for what we do have. God has given us the power, the ability, to decide what to focus our minds on. We can choose to focus our minds on what we do have and what we can do.

Remember the choice in the garden? Humanity was invited to enjoy the fruit from all the trees except one (Genesis 2:16–17). So what happened? We zoomed in on the one that we were not given.

We can now work to undo this part of the curse by enjoying and being satisfied with what God has given us, without demanding more. Part of the power of giving thanks is that it forces our attention onto what is good about something as opposed to what is bad. Even if a situation seems purely bad, we can still give thanks and celebrate since it is shaping our inner being and advancing us on our spiritual journey, while God is working it out in his way and time:

> Consider it pure joy, my brothers and sisters, whenever you face trials of many kinds, because you know that the testing of your faith produces perseverance. Let perseverance finish its work so that you may be mature and complete, not lacking anything. (James 1:2–4)

Being thankful will loosen the tyrannical grip that is imposed by our wants and desires.

Be thankful for existence

People have pointed out the miracle of existence itself. We can be thankful that God exists, that we exist since he created us, and that he loves us and wants us with him.

We can be thankful for our next breath. Our next thought. Our next opportunity to think about God and appreciate his greatness, his goodness, and his love and how he is thinking about you and me at this very moment.

Be thankful for Jesus

We can be thankful for the great love of Christ that compelled him to serve us, sacrifice everything for us, and lay down his life for us. This thought alone should keep us thankful every moment for the rest of our lives.

We can be thankful and focus not on the storms on the outside but the steadfast love and power on the inside.

> *For when once the will*
> *is touched by God himself,*
> *it cannot find contentment*
> *except in the Divinity*
> —St. John of the Cross, A Gloss

Practice: What are some other things that you can be thankful for? What are some of the blessings that you have received? Consider keeping a thankfulness journal and listing each thing.

Break the chains of expectation

Frustration comes from perceiving a gap between what we want and expect versus reality. We often cannot change the reality of our environment and conditions, at least not in the short term. But we can change our expectations. Or perhaps better to say, we can eliminate our expectations.

We demand a lot from ourselves. We can release ourselves and let go of our expectations and the expectations of others. We can cut off the pipeline of discontentment by preventing and stopping our self from judging and preferring.

Practice: Start with small things. Determine that you will be equally happy regardless of the outcome. You may be just as happy and content with slow traffic as fast. Just as happy with one food as another for dinner. Just as happy with your team winning or losing. With getting a call back or not. Think up other things that you can resolve to be happy and content with.

Consciously leave it up to God. Work on being just as happy either way. God knows better.

Ask God to provide for our true needs

If we are struggling with a need or want, we should petition God. He can provide for what we truly need and give us peace for everything else:

> You do not have because you do not ask God. When you ask, you do not receive, because you ask with wrong motives, that you may spend what you get on your pleasures. (James 4:2–3)

> Do not be anxious about anything, but in every situation, by prayer and petition, with thanksgiving, present your requests to God. (Philippians 4:6)

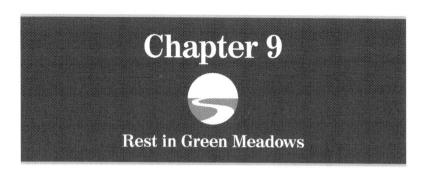

Chapter 9

Rest in Green Meadows

Perhaps it seems a bit odd that we are beginning our journey resting. Aren't we supposed to work first and then rest? Shouldn't we be busy about our journey?

God knows that we need plenty of fuel for the tough parts of the journey that lie ahead.

In Psalm 23, the sheep are resting, lying down: "He makes me lie down in green pastures" (v. 2). And being in green pastures, they are eating as they always are when green grass is available. Because, unlike human food, grass must be eaten almost continuously to get enough to survive.

Have you ever tried to eat grass? If you have, you know that it is very tough and stringy and fibrous. It is very difficult to pulverize and digest. Humans would likely starve with nothing to eat but grass.

Sheep are designed to work with this challenge. Sheep, like cows, have two stomachs. Sheep first bite and tear grass while standing, quickly swallowing it into their first stomach. This first activity of eating is relatively quick. The grass in the first stomach is still in a very raw condition. The real work is yet to be done.

The next step is called chewing the cud. The sheep regurgitate, bring up, the food from the first stomach bit by bit back into their mouth. They then thoroughly chew it and re-swallow it into their second stomach in a much more digestible condition.

When sheep feel safe, like when they are in the presence of a shepherd, they will chew their cud while lying down and resting.

God is offering us nutrition while resting. But how does this help us on our journey to oneness with Christ? To start with, it is part of breaking the curse that separates us from God.

The curse: how and what we eat

As you recall, in the Garden of Eden humanity ate the one thing that God asked us not to eat. The consequence was that we must now struggle to acquire and eat our food.

And what about our spiritual food? Our spiritual food is what feeds and grows and strengthens our souls, what brings us closer to oneness with Christ. Wouldn't it be wonderful if we could receive it without constant struggle?

This is exactly what God has in mind! He says, "Open wide your mouth and I will fill it" (Psalm 81:10). And in doing this for us, he helps to break this element of the curse.

Our spiritual food is God's Word:

. . . man does not live on bread alone but on every word that comes from the mouth of the LORD. (Deuteronomy 8:3)

Whether we read it, listen to it, hear it in worship music, or recall it in our minds, God's Word provides sustenance and nutrition. It feeds, strengthens, encourages, comforts, empowers, builds endurance, and instills hope in our souls.

Deuteronomy 8:3 is such a key verse that Jesus, in an exchange with his enemy when he was in the wilderness without food or water for 40 days, quoted this very scripture. He said, "It is written: 'Man shall not live on bread alone, but on every word that comes from the mouth of God'" (Matthew 4:4).

What is the Word of God?

Most commonly we equate the Word of God to the Holy Bible, Scripture—a collection of documents consisting of words in human language, recorded by about 40 human authors over centuries of time across a wide geographic area, we believe by divine inspiration from God, through the Holy Spirit.

But is the Word of God more than simply words on a page? In the Gospel of John we read:

> In the beginning was the Word, and the Word was with God, and the Word was God. He was with God in the beginning. Through him all things were made; without him nothing was made that has been made. In him was life, and that life was the light of all mankind. The light shines in

the darkness, and the darkness has not overcome it. (John 1:1–5)

This took place long before Scripture was ever recorded. The passage is referring to Jesus Christ. He is the Word made flesh.

This is so important because we can be aware that, when we receive God's Word, we are receiving Jesus, the expression and message and power of God to us. To know this is key for our journey.

What does the Word do?

We tend to think of words almost exclusively as a means to exchange information and grow in knowledge. But the ancient Hebrews and Greeks thought of words as much more. They understood that God's words are his creative power.

In Scripture (Psalm 33:6) and in commentaries on the Torah, we see that "It was with words that God created the world."[6]

The material world was also thought to be created by language in the ancient Greek world. Most of us are somewhat familiar with Pythagoras, since we learned the Pythagorean Theorem in geometry class in school. By recognizing that nature complies with the language, or laws, of mathematics, Pythagoras founded an entire school of thought that held the cosmos was created by this language.

---

[6] Rabbi Dov Linzer, "Words that Create Worlds," *Yeshivat Chovevei Torah* (2016), https://library.yctorah.org/2016/08/words-that-create-worlds/

Now of course at our present time we are much more aware of how words and language are creative. Computer programs and apps create and change material things. DNA is another powerful example. It is the language, the code, for the cells of our bodies.

Jesus is speaking his Word, his truth, his power, his Spirit, to create and build our inner beings, our souls. He created all, sustains all, and is reconciling all to himself, including us:

> For in him all things were created . . . and in him all things hold together . . . and through him to reconcile to himself all things. (Colossians 1:16–20)

What is the purpose of Scripture?

We can start with two things that are not the primary purpose.

In the garden, one of the reasons the fruit was eaten was because it appeared pleasant to the eye and it was anticipated that it would taste good. Sometimes even today God's Word is treated as an avenue to gaining greater worldly wealth or success or enrichment or pleasure. This approach will not bring us any farther on our spiritual journey. Rather, it will hinder us.

A second reason the fruit was eaten was to gain the knowledge of good and evil. According to our enemy, this knowledge would give us power to be as God is. Today we sometimes read God's Word to gain knowledge of good and evil so that hopefully we can choose good. While wisdom from God's Word is very beneficial, it will not help us on our journey if this is our primary purpose for reading it. This is because God explains that his Word, or at least the moral law portion of it, is for the purpose of convicting us of missing the target since we cannot really fix ourselves in our own strength: "What shall we say, then? Is the law sinful? Certainly not! Nevertheless, I would not have known what sin was had it not been for the law. For I would not have known what coveting really was if the law had not said, "You shall not covet." (Romans 7:7).

What is the primary purpose at this stage of the journey? To learn and contemplate two things: (1) the qualities and attributes of God and (2) the promises of God. Why these two things in particular?

We must learn the qualities and attributes of God because, through Christ, he is the one we are uniting with and also the one guiding, leading, and empowering us on our journey as the Good Shepherd. The more we know and appreciate his wonderful attributes, the more we can trust him, follow him, know his will, and love him.

And we must learn what God has done for us and what he promises to do for us because this will give us a vision and lead, inspire, and empower us on our way:

> Your word is a lamp for my feet,
> a light on my path. (Psalm 119:105)

How should we respond to knowledge about God and how he provides for us? Praise him. Praise is knowing and expressing appreciation of the greatness of God. There is power in speaking and proclaiming his greatness and his wonderful qualities. We should also respond by giving thanks for his faithfulness and his promises, even the ones that we do not yet see fulfilled.

God tells us that when we enter the courts of his temple, we should offer praise and thanksgiving:

Enter his gates with thanksgiving
and his courts with praise;
give thanks to him and praise his name.
(Psalm 100:4)

Practice: Whenever you think about God or read and contemplate his Word, give thanks and praise him.

Make an adequate investment

> *The only way to keep a broken vessel full*
> *is to keep it always under the tap.*
> —Billy Sunday

Just as we need to spend adequate time taking enough food into our natural bodies, we need to give adequate space, time, and attention to God's Word.

The Queen of Sheba (Ethiopia) traveled a great distance to visit King Solomon, as he had a great reputation for being blessed by God with great wisdom and riches. She made the trip in order to simply sit at his feet and listen. She was so impressed that she said to him, "How happy your officials, who continually stand before you and hear your wisdom!" (1 Kings 10:8). We can likewise dedicate time and energy to receiving God's Word.

In another example from Scripture, Jesus visited his dear friends Martha, Mary, and Lazarus in their home village of Bethany. While Martha was bustling around with logistical details, Mary sat at the feet of Jesus as he spoke, listening intently. When Martha complained to Jesus that her sister was not helping her, he responded, "Martha, Martha . . . you are worried and upset about many things, but few things are needed—or indeed only one. Mary has chosen what is better, and it will not be taken away from her" (Luke 10:41–42). We can push other trivial details aside and listen to God's Word with rapt attention and total concentration, fully absorbed in him.

Come before him hungry

Just as with physical food, we will take in more of God's Word when we are hungry for it.

Recall when Jesus was literally dying of physical hunger after fasting with no food or water for 40 days in the wilderness. Here is what happened next:

> The tempter came to him and said, "If you are the Son of God, tell these stones to become bread." Jesus answered, "It is written: 'Man shall not live on bread alone, but on every word that comes from the mouth of God.'" (Matthew 4:3–4)

When we find ourselves hungry for so many things in this life, in our outer being, we can then transfer this desire to spiritual hunger. We can think and say, "As much as I desire this thing, God, I want to desire you and your Word even more."

We must come empty-handed, having nothing but our need. We are to be spiritual beggars:

> Blessed are the poor in spirit, for theirs is the kingdom of heaven. (Matthew 5:3)

Practice: Envision coming to God empty and then being filled with his satisfying promises, his wisdom, and the truth of his greatness found in his Word.

We must proclaim our need to God. We must be hungry to receive his nourishment. We must be continuously mindful of the fact that we cannot do it on our own.

Reading and hearing is just the start

Reading or hearing God's Word is good, but the activity of taking it in is just the beginning. Just like the sheep's tearing at the grass and getting it to their first stomach is not the part that really feeds the soul. Rather what is important is the substance that is imported into the soul and given the freedom to bring about change:

> . . . whoever looks intently into the perfect law that gives freedom, and continues in it—not forgetting what they have heard, but doing it—they will be blessed in what they do. (James 1:25)

God's Word is much more than information. We are easily deceived into believing, or typically thinking, of God's Word as good information. Perhaps the best information, but still just information.

Be receptive to God's Word

While God's Word is always true and available, its impact can vary so greatly. Jesus illustrated this powerfully in the following parable:

> A farmer went out to sow his seed. As he was scattering the seed, some fell along the path, and the birds came and ate it up. Some fell on rocky

places, where it did not have much soil. It sprang up quickly, because the soil was shallow. But when the sun came up, the plants were scorched, and they withered because they had no root. Other seed fell among thorns, which grew up and choked the plants. Still other seed fell on good soil, where it produced a crop—a hundred, sixty or thirty times what was sown. (Matthew 13:3–8)

What does this parable mean? Jesus explained:

Listen then to what the parable of the sower means: When anyone hears the message about the kingdom and does not understand it, the evil one comes and snatches away what was sown in their heart. This is the seed sown along the path. The seed falling on rocky ground refers to someone who hears the word and at once receives it with joy. But since they have no root, they last only a short time. When trouble or persecution comes because of the word, they quickly fall away. The seed falling among the thorns refers to someone who hears the word, but the worries of this life and the deceitfulness of wealth choke the word, making it unfruitful. But the seed falling on good soil refers to someone who hears the word and understands it. This is the one who produces a crop, yielding a hundred, sixty or thirty times what was sown. (vv. 18–23)

What makes the difference is how we receive God's Word and how we allow it to build and grow in us. How we nurture and cultivate it. How we contemplate it.

Contemplation

Consider how nutrition feeds and grow muscles. Our bodies work to metabolize the food, converting it to energy and growth, and empowering all the various chemical and electrical processes in our bodies. Back to the example with the sheep—the key to benefitting from the grass's nutrition is dedicating sufficient time and effort to chew the cud. This is similar to how we must take God's Word in and ponder and contemplate and meditate on it.

To do this, we are promised the mind of Christ:

> But we understand these things, for we have the mind of Christ. (1 Corinthians 2:16 NLT)

As we receive God's Word, we can frequently pause to ask God to take control of our minds and enable them to think his thoughts and know his truths. It is his Spirit that leads us into truth and understanding and then translates it into our thought patterns and our behavior patterns and our communication patterns:

> But when he, the Spirit of truth, comes, he will guide you into all the truth. (John 16:13)

As we read or hear Scripture spoken, we must invite Christ in with every word, every phrase, every verse, asking him to reveal and illuminate it and use it to change us. It should sink and lock into us. It should touch us and heal us:

> And we also thank God continually because, when you received the word of God, which you heard from us, you accepted it not as a human word, but as it actually is, the word of God, which is indeed at work in you who believe. (1 Thessalonians 2:13)

Gaining the mind of Christ requires that we make a habit of seeking and searching for the deeper reality in God's Word. There is no special method for this that can be put into words. Inquiring of God, listening quietly, giving the information time to soak in, and getting rid of distractions is the best bet, because ". . . no one knows the thoughts of God except the Spirit of God" (1 Corinthians 2:11).

Over time God will impart to us a different way of looking at things. He will show us that our old way of looking at life is not true and real, and that he has a better way. He can reveal things that are ineffable or really cannot be sufficiently expressed in human words. Divine love, for example, is God's essence and substance that we can never understand through words or rationality or logic. We will only know it when we experience it.

> *Love is an endless mystery,*
> *for it has nothing else to explain it.*
> —Rabindranath Tagore

Speak it back

Jesus spoke God's Word into situations, such as when he spent 40 days in the wilderness (Matthew 4). We mentioned how he responded when he was hungry. His other responses were also insightful and taken directly from Scripture. Note that his answers not only provided truth and information, but they also charted his course and strengthened him in the face of temptation:

> Then the devil took him to the holy city and had him stand on the highest point of the temple. "If you are the Son of God," he said, "throw yourself down. For it is written:

"'He will command his angels concerning you,
and they will lift you up in their hands,
so that you will not strike your foot against a stone.'"

Jesus answered him, "It is also written: 'Do not put the Lord your God to the test.'"

Again, the devil took him to a very high mountain and showed him all the kingdoms of the world and their splendor. "All this I will give you," he said, "if you will bow down and worship me."

Jesus said to him, "Away from me, Satan! For it is written: 'Worship the Lord your God, and serve him only.'"

Then the devil left him, and angels came and attended him. (Matthew 4:5-11)

We can likewise speak God's Word into every situation. We can ask God for help, that he would bring an appropriate verse to our heart and mind at the right time.

Bringing God's Word to life

We can recall God's Word in a way that brings it to life.

Humanity from the beginning of time learned the power of acting out important events and ideas in drama, music, and dancing. This is how primitive tribes passed on truth, values, culture, and legacy. Many in the church today employ this approach in the form of sacraments. The power of celebrating sacraments is that you are rehearsing spiritual realities. It is a reenactment. It can be very powerful if you enter in and mentally become a part of the event.

You can also do this individually. Any time, any place. Everyday things become vehicles for transmitting divine truth and power and substance. Here are a few possible ways you can do this:

When you rise in the morning and face the light, invite God's light to shine on you. He is the light of the world. He shines upon us and illuminates us and enlightens us in his brilliance and glory:

> The path of the righteous is like the morning sun, shining ever brighter till the full light of day. (Proverbs 4:18)

When you bathe, you can feel how he is cleansing you and purifying you and washing you clean from sin and impurities:

> Cleanse me with hyssop, and I will be clean; wash me, and I will be whiter than snow. (Psalm 51:7)

When you get dressed, consider how he is covering you and clothing you in righteousness, dignity, and honor:

> For he has clothed me with garments of salvation and arrayed me in a robe of his righteousness (Isaiah 61:10)

When you eat, remember the words of our Lord at the Last Supper (this is the Eucharist):

> And he took bread, gave thanks and broke it, and gave it to them, saying, "This is my body given for you; do this in remembrance of me."

In the same way, after the supper he took the cup, saying, "This cup is the new covenant in my blood, which is poured out for you." (Luke 22:19–20)

Rest

Rest at the start of a journey makes a big difference. As William Penn said, "True silence is the rest of the mind; it is to the spirit what sleep is to the body, nourishment and refreshment." In this life we must be busy and productive. However, in the realm of the spiritual, we are to be resting:

> By the seventh day God had finished the work he had been doing; so on the seventh day he rested from all his work. Then God blessed the seventh day and made it holy, because on it he rested from all the work of creating that he had done. (Genesis 2:2–3)

Practice: After spending time in and with God's Word, we should give ourselves time just to ruminate and contemplate what God wants to tell us and how he desires to change us.

Our spiritual nutrition is metabolized by God, not by us. We should be silent and open to God, allowing him to speak to us. We should refrain from a quick reaction or judgment. We can afford to give him the space to impart a new and greater understanding and wisdom.

> *Advice is like snow – the softer it falls, the longer it dwells upon, and the deeper it sinks into the mind.*
> —Samuel Taylor Coleridge

What is it that we are feeding on?

We are always feeding our minds and our senses on something.

God is always speaking. Not just directly through his Scripture. He is also speaking into us through his Spirit. Through our conscience. Through worship music, literature, friends, circumstances, and dreams. God's intention is that we continuously feed our minds on this spiritual nourishment.

But the world is also always speaking, attempting to entice us and mislead us into receiving and soaking in its many vain and empty things.

What substance are we feeding on? All the sustenance for our soul should come only from God. He is to be our lot and portion.

God illustrated this point with Ruth. Ruth, a foreigner, traveled to her mother-in-law's wealthy relative, Boaz. Boaz was a kinsman redeemer to Ruth, as Jesus is to us. Here was his advice to Ruth:

> "My daughter, listen to me. Don't go and glean
> in another field and don't go away from here."
> (Ruth 2:8)

We must continuously practice self-control over our minds. We can do this by choosing wholesome and edifying environments and by switching from our natural worldly thoughts to our spiritual thoughts that edify and purify:

> Do not conform to the pattern of this world, but
> be transformed by the renewing of your mind.
> (Romans 12:2)

Let us saturate our minds on all that fits with the following:

> . . . whatever is true, whatever is noble, whatever is right, whatever is pure, whatever is lovely, whatever is admirable—if anything is excellent or praiseworthy—think about such things. (Philippians 4:8)

> *Truth sees God, and wisdom contemplates God,*
> *and from these two comes a third, a holy and*
> *wonderful delight in God, who is love.*
> —Julian of Norwich, *Revelations of Divine Love*

Phase Three: Leading Us

The spiritual journey is not easy. We must travel paths that challenge us and test us. We must face many ups and downs and many struggles. We must learn to submit, obey, endure, and be changed, as Christ is purifying us along the way toward being more like him. This is where the Psalmist says, "He guides me along the right paths for his name's sake" (Psalm 23:3).

What are these paths? They are the major changes that are necessary for us to become more like Christ. Sometimes we may be gladdened as we behold the beauty of God working to transform us. Other times we may feel frustrated and overwhelmed. It can be tough, but it will pay infinite and eternal rewards. It is what we were made for.

Chapter 10

Deciding to step out

We have had a season of receiving and being nourished, strengthened, and built up with God's Word, our spiritual food. But now we begin to grow restless. We feel a yearning for greater progress in our spiritual journey. What is bringing this on?

We are experiencing an internal conflict because we are still stuck with our old self. This is the self that was forged and shaped by the world created by the fall. It is still binding us in chains to old thoughts, old habits, old attitudes, old perspectives.

Now, as our soul expands, it begins bumping up against this old self. The old self is in conflict with God's plan for our new inner being that God is creating in us:

> You were taught, with regard to your former way of life, to put off your old self, which is being corrupted by its deceitful desires; to be made new in the attitude of your minds; and to put on the new self, created to be like God in true righteousness and holiness. (Ephesians 4:22–24)

The truth is sinking in that we do not have space for both the new inner being and the old outer being, the old self. They are not compatible. They are in opposition, creating tension in us:

> For the flesh desires what is contrary to the Spirit,
> and the Spirit what is contrary to the flesh. They
> are in conflict with each other, so that you are not
> to do whatever you want. (Galatians 5:17)

Contemplating the Word of God is like holding up a mirror. We are seeing ourselves in the light of God. We are seeing the many flaws clearly, perhaps for the first time—old urges, desires, and cravings. On the inside we may have pride, jealousy, anger, lust, greed, the need to control things and people, gossip, discontentment, or bad attitudes. On the outside we may have old friends who hold us back, old distractions, old demands that suck us dry, temptations, addictions, bad relationships, and bad habits.

We recognize that deep inside we are still self-seeking. We know that our inner being is not perfect in love of God and our fellow humans. We know that we are not fully at peace but rather continue our struggle to feel good about ourselves, continue to feed our egos and our need to be significant, important, and successful. Our "if only I could have that" or "be that" or "do that" thinking is still alive.

These old traits did not seem bother us so much until now. Or if they did, we did not know what to do about it.

Then God also begins to open our eyes to perceive the deceit and emptiness of this life. What we thought would satisfy us and fulfill us does not. We see the old life for what it really is—temporary and passing away. Empty. Meaningless. It lies to us and insults us each day with promises that do not deliver. It demands that we live up to its standards. It dictates to us what is important and what is not. It has decided for us what is good and what is bad.

Clearly, our former way of life cannot continue. What can we do about it?

> *I have seen all the things that are done under the sun; all of them are meaningless, a chasing after the wind.*
> —Ecclesiastes 1:14

Finish with the world

This world system is feeding our old self. We must get to the point that we are happy to be called by God to reject the love of this life and this world:

> Don't you know that friendship with the world means enmity against God? Therefore, anyone who chooses to be a friend of the world becomes an enemy of God. (James 4:4)

> What good will it be for someone to gain the whole world, yet forfeit their soul? (Matthew 16:26)

It is as with the prodigal son (Luke 15). God brought him to his senses. He remembered the love and kindness and provision of his father and his father's house. Then he looked down at the pig sty and his emaciated condition, at the surrounding filth and squalor, and became painfully aware of his pitiful condition.

> *I was in misery, and misery is the state of every soul overcome by friendship with mortal things and lacerated*

when they are lost. Then the soul becomes aware of the misery
which is its actual condition even before it loses them.
—Augustine of Hippo, *Confessions*

This world is not our home

We must saturate our consciousness with the fact that we do not belong in this world, and we are not designed for this life. We are only passing through on our journey to oneness with Christ:

> But our citizenship is in heaven. And we eagerly await a Savior from there, the Lord Jesus Christ, (Philippians 3:20)

> As it is, you do not belong to the world, but I have chosen you out of the world. (John 15:19)

Practice: Remind yourself and become constantly aware that you are on a journey, that you are a traveler. You are an alien and pilgrim in this world. Your overriding goal is to push on to the destination.

The Patriarchs illustrated this so well:

> By faith he lived as an alien in the land of promise, as in a foreign land, dwelling in tents with Isaac and Jacob, fellow heirs of the same promise; for he was looking for the city which has foundations, whose architect and builder is God. (Hebrews 11:9–10 NASB)

> And Jacob said to Pharaoh, "The years of my pilgrimage are a hundred and thirty. My years

have been few and difficult, and they do not equal the years of the pilgrimage of my fathers." (Genesis 47:9)

What now?

The Good Shepherd leads us forward on his paths. He is the only one who can lead us and protect us and care for us on our way.

In the famous movie *Casablanca*, many people are stuck in the city of that name in Morocco during World War II. A person can only depart for freedom if they can present "letters of transit." I like to think of Jesus, our Good Shepherd, as the only one who can give us the coveted and precious letters of transit on our journey to fulfillment in him.

Chapter 11

Righteousness in the Inner Being

He leads me in the paths of righteousness . . .
—Psalm 23:3

This is the time for us to follow the Good Shepherd as he beckons us toward the paths of righteousness. But how will we know the way? He will lead us and show us:

> Trust in the LORD with all your heart and lean not on your own understanding; in all your ways submit to him, and he will make your paths straight. (Proverbs 3:5–6)

> Whether you turn to the right or to the left, your ears will hear a voice behind you, saying, "This is the way; walk in it." (Isaiah 30:21)

What is this righteousness?

Righteousness is not a word we hear much about during these times. At least not as it was originally intended.

According to Merriam-Webster, the definition of righteousness is "morally right or justifiable."[7]

We may have the impression that being righteous is a matter of complying with a code of what is right and wrong. The problem with this is that it leads us to the mistake of thinking the focus and effort should be on the external, what we do and say. Sadly this puts us on the path of the Pharisees.

Instead, we are called on by God to be available instruments, not free agents making better choices.

That is why God says that we are led on paths of righteousness; it is a process with many twists and turns, hills, and valleys. The paths of righteousness are for us to follow and submit with obedience to our Good Shepherd. This way we will be much more like Christ in our inner being. Then as a natural flow our outer being will also be transformed. In other words, our righteousness on the outside will be the caboose of the train, not the engine.

This chapter addresses the paths in our inner being. The following chapter covers paths for the outer being that will assist us in our journey.

---

[7] "righteous." *Merriam-Webster.com.* 2019. https://www.merriam-webster.com (1 January 2019).

What are these paths?

As we discussed previously, God's Word convicts us. We become aware of the gaps between us and God's Word, specifically the fruit of the Spirit. The fruit of the Spirit is what is produced by God's Spirit in us, as the name indicates. In short, it is God's attributes:

> But the fruit of the Spirit is love, joy, peace, forbearance, kindness, goodness, faithfulness, gentleness and self-control. (Galatians 5:22–23)

God's plan for us on our journey is to manifest his own attributes more and more. The more we become like Christ, the closer we will be to him.

The gaps between our present attributes and God's represent the paths we must travel to become more like Christ.

We should avoid feeling guilty or ashamed of ourselves when we find these gaps. Indulging such feelings will only leave us stuck in our journey, frozen and paralyzed. Instead, we should rejoice when we find them because they afford us the chance to overcome them and thereby draw much closer to Christ.

What should we do with these gaps?

The objective is to swap out our old traits, our old nature, for its true and pure counterparts found in the Fruit of the Spirit. For example, worry and anxiety are the counterparts to peace. Greed and wanting more and covetousness are the counterpart to contentment and satisfaction and giving thanks and appreciation. Anger and hatred and envy are the counterparts to love. Sadness is the counterpart to joy. Discouragement and despair are the counterparts to hope. Doubt is the counterpart to faith. Pride is the counterpart to humility. Lust is the counterpart to purity. Indulgence is the counterpart to self-control.

Swapping can be very difficult. Only God's Spirit in us can make it happen. But it typically does not happen automatically, because part of the solution is on us.

Here are some ways we can begin closing the gaps in our lives:

Start with submitting

Submission. Sadly, the word now can sound oppressive and demeaning. But submission to God is a beautiful thing. Why? Because, only God has the truth and knowledge and power to change us and to advance us on our journey to becoming more like him. In short, submission to what is perfect is a good thing!

Submitting starts with us offering ourselves to God, yielding and surrendering:

> Therefore, I urge you, brothers and sisters, in view of God's mercy, to offer your bodies as a living sacrifice, holy and pleasing to God—this is your true and proper worship. (Romans 12:1)

We talked about this in Chapter 6. But now we are not just offering ourselves up, we are also asking God to have his way in us.

We can contemplate how he is the potter, and we are the clay. We can ask the Lord each day that we might spend time in the potter's house, and that he might form us and shape us:

> So I went down to the potter's house, and I saw
> him working at the wheel . . . shaping [the clay]
> as seemed best to him . . . "Like clay in the hand
> of the potter, so are you in my hand," (Jeremiah
> 18:3–6)

Surrender to God's will

Most of us, even when we believe we live by grace, work at
producing the fruit of the Spirit. We make efforts at being kind,
making good choices, and feeling peaceful, for example. There
is nothing wrong with this. However, it will not take us the full
distance to where we need to go. This is because we are making
efforts in our own strength and our own will.

God's will cannot happen in us and in our lives when we resist
with our own will. We are so accustomed to being in control, it
can be very difficult to let go. In the words of Saint Augustine of
Hippo, "The mind commands the body and is instantly obeyed.
The mind commands itself and meets resistance."

Therefore, we must practice floating in God's will. Without our
own desires and goals and purposes. In God's Spirit. How does
the Holy Spirit operate and take control? Scripture does not say
exactly, but for the New Testament, for today's time, God's Spirit
is compared with three things that reveal its (or his) nature.

One is the breeze:

> The wind blows wherever it pleases. You hear its
> sound, but you cannot tell where it comes from or
> where it is going. So it is with everyone born of the
> Spirit. (John 3:8)

The second is water. Streams of living water. When Jesus talked to the Samaritan woman at the well, he said:

> Everyone who drinks this water will be thirsty again, but whoever drinks the water I give them will never thirst. Indeed, the water I give them will become in them a spring of water welling up to eternal life. (John 4:13–14)

The third is fire, as on the day of Pentecost:

> They saw what seemed to be tongues of fire that separated and came to rest on each of them. (Acts 2:3–4)

All of these metaphors have something in common: they demonstrate the fluid and flowing nature of the Holy Spirit. The Holy Spirit is not something we get and possess, or control, or use as some sort of tool. In fact, quite the opposite. We are to be used and manipulated and flow as the Spirit moves.

We may therefore continuously open ourselves and ask God to pour his Spirit into us. Practice flowing freely in the Spirit. Spend time abandoning unto this. Cultivate floating freely with our eyes on Christ and receiving the Spirit into our inner being. We can then have faith that it is happening, as God promised. He wants to fill us:

> . . . how much more will your Father in heaven give the Holy Spirit to those who ask him! (Luke 11:13)

We may also envision ourselves as columns or rocks in the temple, surrounded and permeated and saturated and infused by God's Spirit, his glory, his love, his presence, and his power:

. . . I will make him a pillar in the temple of My
God. (Revelation 3:12 NASB)

Ask God to enter and occupy

We can cultivate a sense of openness and invite Christ in. To be
our all in all. To have his way in us. He desires to fill us with his
fullness:

> Here I am! I stand at the door and knock. If
> anyone hears my voice and opens the door, I will
> come in and eat with that person, and they with
> me. (Revelation 3:20)

Practice: Envision that you are an empty container. Become
empty. Now God is filling you with himself—his love, his
goodness, his substance. You are in darkness; he is shining his
light into you and changing your darkness to light. Now you ask
him to fill you entirely. To occupy every fiber and cell of your
being. To have his way in you.

> . . . *when Christ the Eternal Sun rises and ascends in our hearts,*
> *so that it is summer in the adornment of our virtues, He gives*
> *His light and His heat to our desires, and draws the heart from*
> *all the multiplicity of earthly things, and brings about unity*
> *and inwardness; and makes the heart grow and bring forth the*
> *leaves of inward love, the flowers of ardent devotion, and the*
> *fruits of thanksgiving and praise, and makes these fruits to*
> *endure eternally, in humble grief, because of our shortcomings.*
> —John of Ruysbroeck, *The Spiritual Espousals*

Change starts with a mirror

Even after submitting and yielding and surrendering, we are likely to find that we still have gaps between our inner being and the fruit of the Spirit.

Much has been said and sung about changing the man or woman or child in the mirror. It is so true. Our job is to be changed first. Then we can change others and our world:

> Why do you look at the speck of sawdust in your brother's eye and pay no attention to the plank in your own eye? How can you say to your brother, "Let me take the speck out of your eye," when all the time there is a plank in your own eye? You hypocrite, first take the plank out of your own eye, and then you will see clearly to remove the speck from your brother's eye. (Matthew 7:3–5)

As we are more and more humble and submitted and honest with ourselves, God opens the door to seeing and knowing our true spiritual state. This is the wisdom that Proverbs speaks of at a deeper level. We become miners of the soul:

> The purposes of a person's heart are deep waters, but one who has insight draws them out. (Proverbs 20:5)

We must search our hearts

As we know from our experience in the garden and what followed, we contain a dangerous combination of wanting more and wanting to be more, even while knowing and obsessing about good and evil, in a sort of twisted fashion. This leads to internal conflict.

Sometimes our wanting more wins out; sometimes our wanting to be good wins out.

This old nature, this old self, flows and spreads and reinforces into all the ingrained, programmed traits that we find difficult to change. These traits are like streams that cut channels in our hearts and minds. As they become very deeply embedded, they morph into strongholds that can be very resistant to change.

We may not even be aware of the scripting that we received from our childhood—our parents and ancestors, community, culture, and education—and carried into our adult lives. The deceitful nature of it is often hidden from us. However, the results and consequences of it are very powerful. All sorts of worries, anxieties, fears, compulsions, negative emotions and thoughts, destructive behaviors, and damaged relationships and the consuming need for power, security, control, and success. In short, while it comes in many forms, it serves to separate us from God. It opposes the will of God in us.

Why doesn't God just deliver us instantly from this? Because he will only go where he is truly invited and welcome. And we can only invite him into the spaces that we are aware of and that we open to him.

So here is what we must do. We must search the self, as it truly is, not as what we want it to be, or pretend it to be, or present it to the world:

> Everyone ought to examine themselves. . .
> (1 Corinthians 11:28)

To be successful and accomplish our purpose, we must skip nothing, hide nothing, and spare nothing. It requires our greatest bravery and courage.

It also requires us to be honest with ourselves. We must guard against justifications and rationalizations and excuses.

Finally, we need to be wise. We can ask God for wisdom, for revelation, for insight, for discernment (Psalm 139:23). Our search with God's help is to be a "light shining in a dark place, until the day dawns and the morning star rises in your hearts" (2 Peter 1:19).

God promises to "open [our] eyes and turn them from darkness to light, and from the power of Satan to God, so that they may receive forgiveness of sins and a place among those who are sanctified by faith in [him]" (Acts 26:18).

> *The passing life of the senses doesn't lead*
> *to knowledge of what our Self is.*
> *When we clearly see what our Self is,*
> *then we shall truly know*
> *our Lord God in great joy.*
> —Julian of Norwich

How do we search?

In order to search our hearts, we must step out of ourselves and observe our self—our thoughts and emotions and desires and feelings and assumptions. For some, this self-inspection and self-evaluation is second nature. For others, though, it is a very new concept. It may be uncomfortable and even frightening. But it is entirely necessary, whatever the cost.

Consider starting by setting aside some time each day to reflect. Maybe at the end of each day. Consider maintaining a journal. We should also try to do it in moments in everyday life as well. But not to the point of driving ourselves crazy!

Work to get in the habit, at any moment in time, of asking, what is going on inside myself? How do I feel? What are my thoughts? Then work to look below the surface for the elements that are driving these thoughts and feelings.

For example, I know I feel angry and frustrated when my schedule is upset by unanticipated demands and situations. What it really is for me is the fear of being out of control.

> *And men go abroad to admire the heights of mountains, the mighty waves of the sea, the broad tides of rivers, the compass of the ocean, and the circuits of the stars, yet pass over the mystery of themselves without a thought.*
> — Augustine of Hippo, *Confessions*

Confronting the gaps

What do we do when we find the things that keep us from bearing the fruit of the Spirit? Understanding the problem isn't enough; we have to solve it. Thankfully, God gives us the necessary methods and tools for addressing gaps.

Realize Jesus is with us in every gap

In every gap, every thought and spoken word, every action, we need to remind ourselves that Jesus is with us. While he is not initiating or causing anything outside of the will of God, he feels all of the fallout, all of the guilt and shame, all of the disappointment, and all of the hurt that we feel.

We can humble ourselves and take every thought captive to him. We can ask him into every situation:

> God made him who had no sin to be sin for us, so
> that in him we might become the righteousness of
> God. (2 Corinthians 5:21)

> For we do not have a high priest who is unable
> to empathize with our weaknesses, but we have
> one who has been tempted in every way, just as
> we are—yet he did not sin. Let us then approach
> God's throne of grace with confidence, so that we
> may receive mercy and find grace to help us in our
> time of need. (Hebrews 4:15–16)

Because he is with us and he has the power, we can seek, desire, and ask for change, not so much for ourselves, but for him and us together. This then is a truly pure desire. We are him, and he is us.

Confess

God already knows our shortfalls. Let us own them.

While we are with Christ in the gap, we must admit these shortfalls to ourselves, to God, and when appropriate and helpful, other people. Without excuses or justifications. Excuses and rationalizations simply keep us from changing, so they are our enemies. Admit it. Speak it. Own it.

To confess means to agree with. We are simply agreeing with God that a particular area of our life needs change. We need him to deliver us from this grip, this habit, this falsehood, this sin, this attitude, this weakness:

> If we confess our sins, he is faithful and just and
> will forgive us our sins and purify us from all
> unrighteousness. (1 John 1:9)

There is no shame in it. God already knows and forgives us, and
he still loves us. But he wants something better for us!

Remember the garden. Humanity saw their nakedness and were
ashamed when God came looking for them. Adam told God, ". . .
I was afraid because I was naked; so I hid" (Genesis 3:10).

Shame and disgrace are feelings that we experience because of what
we hide inside of ourselves. When we admit and acknowledge our
failures, God sets us free. When we have to courage to go through
the process and know and speak the truth, we take away the power
of the problem and the surrounding darkness.

> *. . . we need to fall, and we need to be aware of it;*
> *for if we did not fall, we should not know how weak*
> *and wretched we are of ourselves, nor should we*
> *know our Maker's marvellous love so fully . . .*
> —Julian of Norwich, *Revelations of Divine Love*

See the gap as something to be rid of

We need to see the trait or attitude or thought pattern that is
keeping us from bearing the fruit of the Spirit as something that is
external to our real self. It is not the real us that God has designed.
It is like an unwanted hanger-on.

Once we see it as external to our real self in Christ, we can envision
casting it off and being rid of it:

> Therefore, since we are surrounded by such a great
> cloud of witnesses, let us throw off everything
> that hinders and the sin that so easily entangles.
> (Hebrews 12:1)

We can rejoice that we are being set free from it. Ask God for help
and thank him in advance for making it happen.

Be transformed by God's truth

We must speak God's truth into every gap that we see, over and
over again. It may be a lie we have believed and thought or spoken
a thousand times. Speak God's truth into it a thousand times. By
doing so, we replace the bad, the false, the destructive, with the
good, the truth, the healing and edifying.

Ask for God's help

We can ask God for help. He has promised in what is called the
LORD's prayer to deliver us from evil:

> And lead us not into temptation, but deliver us
> from the evil one. (Matthew 6:13)

We may need to model our asking after the parable of the relentless
widow told by Jesus:

> In a certain town there was a judge who neither
> feared God nor cared what people thought. And
> there was a widow in that town who kept coming
> to him with the plea, "Grant me justice against
> my adversary."

For some time he refused. But finally he said to himself, "Even though I don't fear God or care what people think, yet because this widow keeps bothering me, I will see that she gets justice, so that she won't eventually come and attack me!" (Luke 18:2–5)

Then we can thank God by faith for his deliverance and healing, even if we do not yet see it or feel it. As an example, when I am worrying, I try to repeat to myself over and over, "It is all good in you, Lord Jesus. You are working all things out. Your victory is sure,". Then I begin to thank him.

Walk by faith and not by sight

Here is a powerful verse so often spoken:

For we live by faith, not by sight. (2 Corinthians 5:7)

I always thought of this as trusting God to bring about some desired thing that was not yet visible and apparent.

I now see a different way of living this verse. I should move and transfer my attention and focus from the outer being and the circumstances and situations and conditions of this life and world and instead seek the spiritual dimension in everything. God's hand and heart is behind everything. Not necessarily in the sense that he is causing every little thing to happen but rather in the sense that he is available and gives us the opportunity to seek him, tap into him, and work with him through every situation and in every moment.

This is not something that can be adopted in a formulaic manner or put into words. But with seeking, working, and nurturing we can all learn to practice this.

Manage expectations

Even with all of our efforts and prayers, we will not be made perfect. It is okay. God covers us with his clothes of righteousness. He will see us as clean:

> He has wrapped me in the robe of righteousness
> like a bridegroom with a priest's turban,
> like a bride with her jewels. (Isaiah 61:10 NASB)

We must see ourselves as pure and clean in Christ even as we are seeking cleansing. Our inner being is pure where God resides even as the construction and maintenance crews are toiling diligently on the exterior structure.

At the end of this process, by God's faithfulness, we will hopefully have a core in our soul that is like Christ. He will "delete" the rest in his time:

> He has made everything beautiful in its time.
> (Ecclesiastes 3:11)

Keep our eyes on the prize

1 Corinthians 9:24 tells us that we should persevere like a runner in a race; we should strive after the prize:

Do you not know that in a race all the runners run, but only one gets the prize? Run in such a way as to get the prize.

The prize is divine love in Christ. We are not producing the fruit of the Spirit, or shall we say the Spirit is not producing the fruit, for the purpose of simply being good. That would only make us good Pharisees. We are producing so that we may love Christ better. By becoming more like him, I can better pursue him.

Chapter 12

Righteousness in the Outer Being

What is happening in our outer being while we are walking the pathways of righteousness in our inner being?

The outer being is a good servant but a horrible master. It is a big part of why our souls are so empty and vacuous at the time we start our journey.

How can we turn things around and make our outer being, our life in this world, a servant and support and help to our spiritual journey?

Remove expectations

It seems that a common misperception is that we will ultimately be victorious and successful in our outer being, in our life in this world. This mistaken way of thinking will destroy our inner journey to oneness in Christ. We need to remember that Jesus was not victorious in this life. In fact, quite the contrary. We are called to follow in his steps and therefore should not anticipate anything different. Things in this life are probably not going to work out. And it is okay. We have eternity with Christ, that is all that matters.

Deal with anything big

We need to deal with anything really big first before we can make much progress on our journey. Please ask yourself whether there is anything that is controlling and dominating your life to such a degree that you cannot focus on listening to God and being open to change. If so, it must be dealt with immediately, just as you cannot proceed with physical training until you deal with a major injury.

How we deal with such hindrances varies by situation. Just to name a few examples, it may be that we need to apologize and seek forgiveness from someone who hurt us deeply. We may need to get in rehab and a 12-step group for addiction. It may be that we need to admit to a crime and suffer the consequences. It may be a mental illness that requires medical help for. It may be counseling for trauma we have experienced. Please keep in mind that it may or may not be something that is considered big in the eyes of the world. Only you can judge the impact it is having on you and your ability to make your spiritual journey.

Please get help and find healing and deliverance as soon as possible. This should take priority.

Trim and simplify

We have limited time and energy. Our lives are so busy already. We must scale back and become content with only what is necessary among material things, busyness, and activities to keep us going:

But if we have food and clothing, we will be content with that. (1 Timothy 6:8)

By doing this, we will give ourselves as much time and energy to direct toward our spiritual growth as possible.

This can be achieved by undertaking a personal inventory of our possessions and commitments. How are they impacting our spiritual journey? It does not have to be "sin" for it to distract and drain us.

Let us consider what changes we need to make. Maybe we need to change jobs. Drop habits. End or change relationships. It may be difficult and require sacrifice, but it will be so worth it as we come closer to Christ. Of course, we must use wisdom to make these changes, conducting and communicating in a way that avoids hurting others or violating oaths.

Serve Christ by loving and serving people

One of the greatest and most powerful means of being freed from our own desires and cravings is to switch tracks and be about God's business, as Jesus did:

> For I have come down from heaven not to do my will but to do the will of him who sent me. (John 6:38)

Find ways to serve, ways to help. God has already planned good works for us to perform in love:

> For we are God's handiwork, created in Christ Jesus to do good works, which God prepared in advance for us to do. (Ephesians 2:10)

What is this good work? It is living out Christ's new command:

> A new command I give you: Love one another. As
> I have loved you, so you must love one another. By
> this everyone will know that you are my disciples,
> if you love one another. (John 13:34–35)

Practice: Each moment, think "I am on duty and mission with God. What is it that I believe he would have me do?" All results are his.

Of course, as mentioned previously, even good works should not be done in such excess as to damage our journey in the inner being. Jesus always set aside plenty of time for his spiritual connection with his Father in heaven.

Breaking the chains of self-interest – actions without rewards

Recall the consequence in the garden relating to self-interest:

> By the sweat of your brow
> you will eat your food (Genesis 3:19)

This created our dominant system of effort-achieve-reward. The outer being is characterized by doing. We typically shape our actions, words, and relationships for the purpose of achieving success and receiving rewards. We may not think about it or express it in such a self-serving manner. But even our good deeds of service may be done for a reward. Rewards are both extrinsic and intrinsic. For example, we may get an education so we can get an interesting and well-paying job. Intrinsically it may make us feel successful. Or we may do volunteer work and enjoy the recognition or feel intrinsically good about helping others.

We may or may not be conscious of the effort-achieve-reward system. But it is likely operating in our lives. We can recognize this without needing to feel bad about it. It is just the way that our world works.

We can redeem and undo this aspect of the curse when we do works and actions without anticipating or receiving any reward, other than perhaps pleasing God. This frees us up so that although we do work, it is without the struggle. We help and serve those whom we have no expectation or desire that they return a favor. Without recompense or acknowledgement.

Expect no reward. Do not accept a reward if one is offered from a wrong source or to be used for wrong purposes. We can be like Abram (God changed Abram's name to Abraham later). After rescuing hostages from evil leaders of cities such as Sodom and Gomorrah, Abram refused to accept any payment or award. He had the following to say:

> I will accept nothing belonging to you, not even
> a thread or the strap of a sandal, so that you
> will never be able to say, "I made Abram rich."
> (Genesis 14:23)

If you do receive an external reward, as might be required out of courtesy, be gracious on the outside. But on the inside, guard against feeding your ego or self-esteem or sense of goodness. On the inside, treat it as though you did not receive it. Refuse any attachment in your heart to it.

Similarly, guard against going out and helping those in need and then returning to church or fellowship group or family gatherings or the office and bragging about it. Or "sharing" about it. Praise from others is a coveted reward in itself, isn't it? Do your service and blessing quietly, humbly, in secret. Tell no one. Finish, go home quietly, and say no more.

Our efforts should be to help and bless the least. Those most in need. Those whom cannot help us in return in any manner:

> Then Jesus said to his host, "When you give a luncheon or dinner, do not invite your friends, your brothers or sisters, your relatives, or your rich neighbors; if you do, they may invite you back and so you will be repaid. But when you give a banquet, invite the poor, the crippled, the lame, the blind, and you will be blessed. Although they cannot repay you, you will be repaid at the resurrection of the righteous." (Luke 14:12–14)

This includes the poor in every manner. Those poor financially. Those with no social status. Those without success. Those discouraged, weak, empty, lonely, unpopular. And even those difficult to deal with.

This is not to be something we do with extra time left over from doing all the things that do provide a benefit. This should be at the core of our efforts.

Sacrifice

We will go through tough times. We will be treated unfairly. Maligned. Slandered. Hurt. Inconvenienced.

Almost everyone experiences hardship. It is a given in life for those who are pursuing the spiritual journey, and for those who are not. It is how we handle it that makes all the difference. That is why

God has told us this, saying through Peter, "Dear friends, do not be surprised at the fiery ordeal that has come on you to test you, as though something strange were happening to you. But rejoice inasmuch as you participate in the sufferings of Christ, so that you may be overjoyed when his glory is revealed" (1 Peter 4:12–13).

We can give thanks through tough times.

Perhaps one of the greatest blessings is that hardships give us the opportunity to join Christ in suffering, sorrow, disappointment, pain, tiredness. It becomes a powerful bridge and connection with him. It is where we find him.

> *Only the wounded*
> *Understand the agonies of the wounded*
> —Mirabai, "I Am Mad With Love"

Start sacrificing these losses and failure and hurts to Christ. Start with the small things, the everyday things. Start with a minor headache. Heavy traffic. The lost game or promotion. The cross word spoken by a parent or sibling or child or friend. Give it to Christ. Give thanks in it and through it. Rejoice. Christ suffered greatly. He wants us to share our suffering with him. It will help us on our journey:

> . . . we share in his sufferings in order that we may also share in his glory. (Romans 8:17)

> I want to know Christ—yes, to know the power of his resurrection and participation in his sufferings, becoming like him in his death (Philippians 3:10)

When you receive less than what is deserved, instead of complaining, make it a sacrifice for God.

> *In this world there is no fruitfulness without*
> *suffering—either physical pain, secret sorrow,*
> *or trials known sometimes only to God.*
> —Thérèse de Lisieux

Without complaining

Philippians 2:14 says that we should do everything—the enjoyable as well as the difficult things in life—without complaining: "Do everything without complaining and arguing."

At first it might require plenty of self-control, grit, and determination to avoid complaining when we face hardships. But then, as we understand and believe that all things we are tempted to complain about are temporary and of no importance, we can release complaining naturally:

> What, then, shall we say in response to these things? If God is for us, who can be against us? (Romans 8:31)

> Do everything without grumbling or arguing, so that you may become blameless and pure, "children of God without fault in a warped and crooked generation." Then you will shine among them like stars in the heavens. (Philippians 2:14–15)

Small works and blessings

Only small works, acts of service, and blessings can be done many times a day regardless of who you are and what you do. Do the smallest of things with the greatest of love. This may advance your journey the most. It is not the size of the work but the heart it is done with that matters.

Think about opportunities to bless and serve. Our thoughts will then be on others rather than ourselves. We have the opportunity to communicate a blessing in practically every situation. A smile. A word of kindness. A good wish. A small gift. A helping hand.

Do all things unto Christ

God is omnipresent; he sees and is everywhere. He never leaves us. We know this from knowing his nature and from verses such as this:

> "Where can I go from your Spirit?
> Where can I flee from your presence?
> If I go up to the heavens, you are there;
>   if I make my bed in the depths, you are there.
> If I rise on the wings of the dawn,
>   if I settle on the far side of the sea,
> even there your hand will guide me,
>   your right hand will hold me fast.
> (Psalm 139:7–10)

So he knows and experiences everything we do. But even more than this astounding fact, he receives and is impacted by our every action and takes it very personally. We know this from the verse we mentioned earlier, when Jesus spoke of the judgment in Matthew 25:35–40: "For I was hungry and you gave me something to eat, I was thirsty and you gave me something to drink, I was a stranger and you invited me in, I needed clothes and you clothed me, I was sick and you looked after me, I was in prison and you came to visit me."

When the people asked him when they had done these things, Jesus answered, "Truly I tell you, whatever you did for one of the least of these brothers and sisters of mine, you did for me" (v. 40).

Everything we do we do to God. And we will receive a report card! Therefore we should commit and do all things to and for Christ. Every breath, every thought, every action, every word, every gesture:

> Commit to the LORD whatever you do, and he
> will establish your plans. (Proverbs 16:3)

Practice: Envision turning over every situation, activity, and problem to Christ. He gladly reaches out and receives it from you in love.

Change your relationship with nature – see the beauty

What is your relationship like with nature? With God's creation— the sun, the moon, the stars, the earth, mountains, valleys, rivers, streams, oceans, lakes, ponds, forests, grass, the tree outside your window?

I pretty much ignored or viewed objects as material things to be manipulated. Now I am changing the way I view things, particularly nature. I try and stop and spend a moment viewing and appreciating the beauty of God's artwork.

Back to the garden. Having fallen, humanity was made to struggle for food from the field (Genesis 3:17). With painful toil, we became too busy to enjoy God's creation and beauty. Instead it became all about getting and using and consuming material and non-material things.

When we realize how we have been deceived into passing over God's beauty, we can let go of our strivings and instead just behold and enjoy God's glory in what he has created.

> *All praise be yours, my Lord, through all that you have made,*
> *And first my lord Brother Sun,*
> *Who brings the day; and light you give to us through him.*
> *How beautiful is he, how radiant in all his splendor!*
> *Of you, Most High, he bears the likeness.*
> *All praise be yours, my Lord, through Sister Moon and Stars;*
> *In the heavens you have made them, bright*
> *And precious and fair.*
> *All praise be yours, My Lord, through Brothers Wind and Air,*
> *And fair and stormy, all the weather's moods,*
> *By which you cherish all that you have made.*
> *All praise be yours, my Lord, through Sister Water,*
> *So useful, lowly, precious and pure.*
> —St. Francis of Assisi

Change your relationship with time

God has designed a rhythm to life. We see it in the heavens, in the seasons, even in the circadian rhythm of the 24-hour cycle:

> There is a time for everything,
> and a season for every activity under the heavens:
> (Ecclesiastes 3:1)

God has a flow, a rhythm, a pace that allows us to live in peace. He tells us, "Take my yoke upon you and learn from me, for I am gentle and humble in heart, and you will find rest for your souls. For my yoke is easy and my burden is light." (Matthew 11:29–30). When we yoke ourselves to Jesus, we must walk and live at his pace. And he was never in a hurry, never in a rush. Adopting his pace and joining in his flow is part of submitting and yielding to God.

Change your relationship with your body

God has given us our physical bodies as a gift. Therefore, we should always give thanks. God designed our bodies, along with our minds, to be our servants in our outer being.

In the garden, as mentioned earlier, humanity's eyes were opened and we hid from God because we were naked and felt ashamed because of it (Genesis 3:10). The truth is, though, that God made our bodies to be our helpers, and they are beautiful in his eyes.

We need to remember that every message that criticizes and condemns our bodies is a lie. The enemy of our souls manipulates us to be discontent. We must not fall for these tricks and deceit. Instead, we need to constantly remind ourselves that our bodies are gifts from God. He is pleased with our bodies. We are to be also. What else matters?

Practice: Be still and present your body to God. Feel a breath and know it is a good gift from God and enjoy it. Rehearse giving every organ and cell to God to occupy through his Spirit. Feel him lift up your body and fill it with his light and lightness of being.

Give it back to him. He wants it. He does not see it at all as we do, through the lenses of social messages, cues, and pressure:

> Therefore, I urge you, brothers and sisters, in view of God's mercy, to offer your bodies as a living sacrifice, holy and pleasing to God—this is your true and proper worship. (Romans 12:1)

Unfortunately, for so many of us our bodies have taken on entirely different roles. Out of a corrupted view of our bodies has flowed negative body image, a deadly desire to be "perfect," jealousy, insecurity, arrogance, conceit, narcissism, and lust.

But we can remind ourselves that our bodies are temples of God. His Spirit dwells in us:

> Do you not know that your bodies are temples of the Holy Spirit, who is in you, whom you have received from God? You are not your own; you were bought at a price. Therefore honor God with your bodies. (1 Corinthians 6:19–20)

Practice: Be silent and feel your body simply exist. Be aware of it without thinking any thoughts of judgment or desire or condemnation or vanity or discontent. Now look up and ask God to take it, have it, possess it, and use it. Thank God for it. As it is. Ask God to liberate you from all of the false outside and inside lies about it. Ask God to help you take care of it in his grace and will, since it is a valued servant to you and to God and to others you serve.

There have been many good books written on this subject, and there are many good therapists who specialize in it. Be sure to find help if you continue to struggle with your body image.

Phase Four: Testing Us

The fourth phase, the testing phase, is when all appears lost and we are tempted to feel despair. We are tested to determine if we will stay true to Christ and hold on to him for dear life. We ask ourselves, is he truly my everything? Will we sacrifice and give up everything to gain oneness with him?

He upholds us, comforts us, as we cling to him. He comforts us in a way that no one and nothing else can. He calms the storm. He takes us into a peaceful place. He catches us as we fall into him.

Chapter 13

The Valley

At times in our spiritual journey we will come to "the valley of the shadow of death." The best translation may be "valley of greatest darkness" rather than "death." It is cut off by mountains. It is narrow. The Psalmist may have been thinking of the many narrow canyons in Israel that can be found with nearly vertical walls of rock on either side.

These valleys are dark, desolate, arid, dead. They are where God calls us to strip away all other things, even what we believe we are doing for him, and just reach out and cling to him. He alone is sufficient. He alone satisfies. He alone fulfills. We remember that Jesus, at the cross, lost even his clothes. He was entirely destitute of all things in this world. He was left with nothing.

Even though I walk through the valley of the shadow of death,
I will fear no evil,
for you are with me;
your rod and your staff, they comfort me.
—Psalm 23:4

What the valley means for our spiritual journey

Up to this point in our journey we have learned many things, but we have not made it all the way to knowing God as he is in himself. We know and experience many of his beautiful qualities that emanate and flow from him. Much as the sun sends out light that warms us, allows us to see, and produces food for us. But this light streaming from the sun to our planet is not the sun as it is in itself.

We are not able to reach and dwell in the sun to experience it as it is in itself. Not as we are today. Not just because it is a great distance away, but because it is far too hot—almost 10,000°F! We could only enter the sun if we were adapted and changed for the environment.

This is what God does. He brings us into and through the valley for the purpose of changing and transforming us so that we can then experience him, as he is in himself, or at least in a much more real and powerful and deep and intimate and profound state. Beyond all we can ask or imagine.

Picture the valley as a bridge to Christ. Or as one of the theoretical wormholes that bridge from one universe to another.

Reversing the curse

To understand the valley experience better, once again we are taken back to the garden where we rejected and disconnected from God.

In the garden, we were given much. Food. Water. Light. All that we needed:

> Now the LORD God had planted a garden in the
> east, in Eden; and there he put the man he had
> formed. The LORD God made all kinds of trees
> grow out of the ground—trees that were pleasing
> to the eye and good for food. . . . A river watering
> the garden flowed from Eden; (Genesis 2:8–10)

But sadly, we decided that all of these blessings were not enough.
We just could not do without the one thing he asked us to forego:
fruit from the tree of the knowledge of good and evil.

Now, fast forward to our spiritual journey. He brings us into the
valley of great darkness. The barren and dark canyons are quite
the opposite of the garden. Dry, desolate, dark. He has taken away
everything except two slender trees, his staff and rod. Things
are quite the reverse from in the garden, where we could have
everything except the one tree.

What do the staff and rod that we grab hold of represent? Jesus's
death on the cross. The cross correlates with the trees in the
center of the garden. By dying Jesus removed the penalty from
the knowledge of good and evil that brought judgment:

> "He himself bore our sins" in his body on the
> cross, so that we might die to sins . . . (1 Peter 2:24)

By rising he restored the tree of life everlasting:

> Praise be to the God and Father of our Lord Jesus
> Christ! In his great mercy he has given us new
> birth into a living hope through the resurrection
> of Jesus Christ from the dead (1 Peter 1:3)

In the valley, we have the glorious opportunity to make a different decision than the one made in the garden. We can decide to be content and satisfied and thankful with giving up all if we can only have his staff and rod that comfort us. We look for nothing else; we want nothing else.

With him, we are once again reversing the curse!

How do we enter and transit the valley?

This stage is a bit different. The previous stages could be entered and started pretty much when we felt we were ready. And while God granted us the victory in each stage, much of it at least appeared to be due to our efforts. But now he leads us into, and through, the valley. We must only submit and cooperate.

But there is much that we can do to prepare for the valley experience. And we can ask him to make it happen. We can start by understanding the valley better.

Instances of darkness in Scripture

While darkness in Scripture typically signifies evil, spiritual deadness, and the absence of God, there is another type of darkness. This other type of darkness is something we must pass through as an access point to God, where we are stripped of other things and prepared to enter into his presence. The following are some examples from the Bible of this type of darkness.

Moses

Moses was the leader of the Israelites as God delivered them from slavery and brought them out of Egypt. Since they were God's people and were now to be their own nation, God would give them the Old Testament law to instruct them on how to live and operate.

God first gave the law by speaking it (later it would be written on stone tablets). For this great revelation, Moses had to pass through darkness on Mount Sinai. In a powerful moment, Moses met with God after he climbed Mount Sinai through darkness:

> The people remained at a distance, while Moses approached the thick darkness where God was. (Exodus 20:21)

Ruth

Ruth, a widow, alien, and foreigner, accompanied by her mother-in-law, traveled to the estate of her mother-in-law's wealthy kinsman, Boaz. He permitted her to glean in his fields and dwell on his property. One night she followed the tradition at the time for requesting to become someone's servant. Boaz was sleeping on the threshing floor at the height of harvest. In the darkness Ruth climbed down onto the threshing floor and lay down at his feet:

> Ruth approached quietly, uncovered his feet and lay down. In the middle of the night something startled the man; he turned—and there was a woman lying at his feet!

"Who are you?" he asked.

"I am your servant Ruth," she said. "Spread the corner of your garment over me, since you are a guardian-redeemer of our family."

"The Lord bless you, my daughter," he replied. "This kindness is greater than that which you showed earlier: You have not run after the younger men, whether rich or poor. And now, my daughter, don't be afraid. I will do for you all you ask. All the people of my town know that you are a woman of noble character." (Ruth 3:7–11)

And he ended up doing even more by marrying her, and she was in the direct line of King David and of Jesus's human lineage!

Jacob

As Jacob traveled back to his home, the night before he was to arrive and meet his brother Esau, who had every reason to hate him, he sent his family and servants and possessions ahead of him and dwelled alone in the dark. Here is what happened:

So Jacob was left alone, and a man wrestled with him till daybreak. When the man saw that he could not overpower him, he touched the socket of Jacob's hip so that his hip was wrenched as he wrestled with the man. Then the man said, "Let me go, for it is daybreak."

But Jacob replied, "I will not let you go unless you bless me."

The man asked him, "What is your name?"

"Jacob," he answered.

Then the man said, "Your name will no longer be Jacob, but Israel, because you have struggled with God and with humans and have overcome."

Jacob said, "Please tell me your name."

But he replied, "Why do you ask my name?" Then he blessed him there.

So Jacob called the place Peniel, saying, "It is because I saw God face to face, and yet my life was spared." (Genesis 32:24–30)

With a new name and a new identity, Jacob entered into his destiny.

Jesus

The sky was darkened when Jesus died on the cross:

At noon, darkness came over the whole land until three in the afternoon. (Mark 15:33)

This darkness lasted on the earth until the moment Jesus died on the cross. And then after Jesus died, he was banished for three days into the utter darkness and lowness of the underworld.

> What does "he ascended" mean except that he
> also descended to the lower, earthly regions?
> (Ephesians 4:9)

The Apostles Creed expresses it this way:

> [Jesus] . . . was crucified, died, and was buried.
> He descended into hell; on the third day He arose
> again from the dead . . .

And in another instance, shortly after Jesus was crucified, two of
Jesus's disciples were walking on the road to a village by the name
of Emmaus. Someone they did not recognize caught up to them
and walked alongside. With not much to do but walk, the disciples
began a conversation with this stranger. And then, as night began
to fall, they invited the stranger to stop with them at a nearby inn
and have dinner.

Here is what happened:

> But they urged him strongly, "Stay with us, for it
> is nearly evening; the day is almost over." So he
> went in to stay with them. When he was at the
> table with them, he took bread, gave thanks, broke
> it and began to give it to them. Then their eyes
> were opened and they recognized him, [Jesus!]
> and he disappeared from their sight. They asked
> each other, "Were not our hearts burning within
> us while he talked with us on the road and opened
> the Scriptures to us?" (Luke 24:29–32)

Paul

The Apostle Paul, who was violently persecuting Christians, was traveling on the road to Damascus, when he was struck with a great light that temporarily blinded him:

> Saul got up from the ground, but when he opened his eyes he could see nothing. So they led him by the hand into Damascus. For three days he was blind, and did not eat or drink anything. (Acts 9:8–9)

Being blind, he essentially dwelled in darkness. He then believed and decided to follow and serve Christ.

The spiritual valley

In the valley, we are called to undergo a type of crucifixion and dying to ourselves:

> But rejoice inasmuch as you participate in the sufferings of Christ, so that you may be overjoyed when his glory is revealed. (1 Peter 4:13)

> We were therefore buried with him through baptism into death in order that, just as Christ was raised from the dead through the glory of the Father, we too may live a new life. (Romans 6:4)

> Now if we died with Christ, we believe that we will also live with him. (Romans 6:8)

We must die to self, the old self, and this life and this world:

> For you died, and your life is now hidden with
> Christ in God. (Colossians 3:3)

This process is the darkness.

What is the meaning of dying to self? I always thought of dying with Christ as enduring a set of tough circumstances that were thrust upon us. We think of suffering as extreme pain. The kind of pain that we experience in our outer being. Such as being nailed to a cross.

This is not the sort of pain that is primarily experienced in the valley, though.

Instead, the darkness and dying we are to undergo requires losing all attachment and involvement and connection with everything, even in our inner being, except our connection with the crucified Christ (staff and rod).

St. John of the Cross speaks about this in terms of light being extinguished:

> for even if I have no light
> I have the life of heaven.
> For the blinder love is
> the more it gives such life,
> holding the soul surrendered,
> living without light in darkness.

The light that is extinguished is the light of these attachments, even attachments to good things. It is not necessarily a loss in our outer being; we will still have families, friends, jobs, and the like. Instead, it is our attachments to all of these things in our inner being, the connections and channels to them, that are to be severed.

We are to run on autopilot in our outer being in a sense. We run on faith alone, the kind that believes even while not seeing or experiencing.

We shall effectively extinguish every other desire and priority and value. We continuously renounce, relinquish, and detach from all things in our heart and soul.

> *My life is like a faded leaf,*
> *My harvest dwindled to a husk:*
> *Truly my life is void and brief*
> *And tedious in the barren dusk;*
> *My life is like a frozen thing,*
> *No bud nor greenness can I see:*
> *Yet rise it shall–the sap of Spring;*
> *O Jesus, rise in me.*
> —Christina Rossetti, "A Better Resurrection"

We must want it

God will only bring us through the valley if we truly believe to the bottom of our core that our one and only desire is to be one with Christ and that we will happily lose everything else. We must mentally agree with this. Then we must continuously ask for it and hope for it and look for it.

We can reach the point of genuinely wanting to lose and be liberated from everything except Christ by considering them entirely worthless:

> But whatever were gains to me I now consider loss
> for the sake of Christ. What is more, I consider
> everything a loss because of the surpassing worth
> of knowing Christ Jesus my Lord, for whose sake
> I have lost all things. I consider them garbage,
> that I may gain Christ and be found in him,
> (Philippians 3:7–9)

We can envision all things washing away. Disappearing.

> *One does not discover new lands without consenting*
> *to lose sight of the shore for a very long time.*
> — André Gide

We cling to the crucified Christ

As we let go of our old self, we must cling to God. We must cast
ourselves upon Christ and cling to his staff and his rod:

> . . . your rod and your staff, they comfort me.
> (Psalm 23:4)

This fits with what God says in other parts of his Word, such as,
". . . you shall serve Him [God] and cling to Him" (Deuteronomy
10:20).

The staff and rod represent a narrow connection with God. We
shall have a steadfast, exclusive, and consuming focus on him,
holding on to him for dear life as a life preserver in the wind and
waves and darkness.

To our human nature this does not seem reasonable at all. What happened to the success, the glory, and the happiness that were promised?

But the divine love now in our souls understands it and knows it differently. We now want to have intimacy with Christ where he has been. In the valley and darkness. We want to share his fullness with him, or perhaps we should say share his emptiness with him.

> *Do not think that he who lives*
> *the so-precious inner life*
> *finds joy and gladness*
> *in the sweetness of the earth;*
> *but there beyond all beauty*
> *and what is and will be and was,*
> *he tastes I-don't-know-what*
> *which is so gladly found.*
> —St. John of the Cross, A Gloss

We can only live with him if we die with him first:

> I want to know Christ—yes, to know the power of his resurrection and participation in his sufferings, becoming like him in his death, and so, somehow, attaining to the resurrection from the dead. (Philippians 3:10–11)

I previously thought the spiritual journey would be a fairly steady incline to heaven. I thought this was where God resided, this was where we would find him. This was where we would share in his glory and greatness. We would ascend to him.

But no, we must first go down low in the valley, into the darkness. This is where we meet him, so that he can then bring us up to a higher place:

> And so Jesus also suffered outside the city gate to make the people holy through his own blood. Let us, then, go to him outside the camp, bearing the disgrace he bore. (Hebrews 13:12–13)

We must by faith accept him and cling to him and pursue him and walk with him and follow him. Even when we cannot see him or hear him or see the path. We must totally trust him with full surrender and submission. All we can sense and perceive is his staff and rod. And now, when we are tempted to have more and know more, we do not give in as we did in the garden, but instead cling only to him even tighter with faithfulness.

It is a step of faith we are gambling that the Shepherd is here for us. He will find us and guide us and be with us in the darkness. We let go of the ground and surrounding walls. Now, will he catch us as we fall?

Practice: In your devotion time, in your mind and soul, find the deepest part of God that you can focus on and connect with. Hold on to this for as long as possible. Practice this more and more often and seek to go deeper and deeper. This is hard to describe in words, so you must make your way on this with God's help.

After the leap

How will we feel while we are in the valley? Will we feel God's presence with us?

Not necessarily. We may feel nothing. Darkness and nothingness and emptiness. We have given up everything for God. And he appears not to be with us! The staff and rod are the only clues that he even exists and is with us. This is just our faith and hope in him. This is the dark night of the soul spoken of by the saints of old.

So how does this leave us? Feeling broken and empty. In anguish. Unworthy. Perhaps numb. Like Jesus in the Garden of Gethsemane on the night he was betrayed.

However, we must somehow not focus on the darkness. If we do, we will be defeated utterly. Instead we focus all on Jesus's staff and rod. We cling to it. His promise of divine love. The hope and faith we have in this. We continue to overflow in love toward him. Thanks to God, we remember his faithfulness.

Why is all of this necessary?

What is going on here? Why would a loving God do this? And why would it be necessary or helpful?

Here it is—it is the final reversal of the sin and curse from the garden. In the garden we rejected God and turned our back on him for self-gain. But despite this he stayed true to us. Now we are blessed with the opportunity to lose everything and even feel that we are rejected by God, and yet stay true to him. This is the final and ultimate culmination and spiritual triumph. It is what Jesus did on the cross. Indeed, we are following Jesus in his steps. Then we will be able to stand with him in eternal victory!

Only when we cease from being connected or valuing activity, physical or mental, can we be in a state to receive God. We are open when we are resting and allowing, indeed inviting, God to work in us and fill us and transform us.

Another way of looking at it is— he will only come into us to the degree that we become vacant. Like a jar must be emptied of liquid to make room for a gas.

God is performing the final purification on us. Yet we know it not since we unable to accurately perceive our surroundings, our progress, or God.

> *Never stop just because you feel defeated. The journey to*
> *the other side is attainable only after great suffering.*
> —Santosh Kalwar, *Quote Me Everyday*

What is happening in our outer being?

Logistically we continue on. At this point we are programmed to do the right thing. To perform good works. To serve and love and help and bless. We continue to do all of these things. We have become faithful in the small things, our outer being.

Although we have died to our outer being, God is faithful through our new programming and righteousness. Now our inner being, sufficiently purified, flows into the outer being. We do God's will without the need to focus on it. Goodness flows out naturally by God's plan from the beginning, without our struggling to battle with good and evil.

> *The ego hates losing – even to God.*
> —Richard Rohr, *Falling Upward:*
> *A Spirituality for the Two Halves of Life*

To arrive where you are, to get from where you are not,
You must go by a way wherein there is no ecstasy.
In order to arrive at what you do not know
You must go by a way which is the way of ignorance.
In order to possess what you do not possess
You must go by the way of dispossession.
In order to arrive at what you are not
You must go through the way in which you are not. . .
—T.S. Eliot

Phase Five: Redeeming Us

At last we reach the final phase in our spiritual journey, when God rewards us and gives us a new life and brings us into full union with Christ in divine love. He lavishes his love and blessings on us. We stumbled many times, but he rewards us nonetheless. This is where the Psalmist says, "You prepare a table before me in the presence of my enemies. You anoint my head with oil; my cup overflows. Surely your goodness and love will follow me all the days of my life, and I will dwell in the house of the Lord forever" (Psalm 23:5–6).

We earn none of this, but there is much we can do to be prepared to receive. There is grace in receiving well, just as there is grace in giving well.

Chapter 14

Banquet Table

Immediately following Psalm 23:4, we see a dramatic shift in scenery:

> You prepare a table before me
> in the presence of my enemies; (v. 25)

Everything has changed. God is now leading us out of the dark valley and into God's glorious divine radiance:

> For he has rescued us from the dominion of darkness and brought us into the kingdom of the Son he loves, (Colossians 1:13)

Notice that the Shepherd is no longer referred to as "he." Now we refer to him as "you." Because we now know him personally.

We have a new and transformed relationship. We have been changed from lowly sheep into people who know Christ, the Good Shepherd, intimately.

And now we have moved from feeding and drinking in the pasture and stream to dining at a banquet table and from a beautiful cup. Our eyes are opened. God reveals himself. We have been transformed. God looks different because we are different.

Undoing the curse

I often wondered why it is said that the table is prepared in the presence of our enemies. The explanation lies, once again, in the garden. Recall that we ate the forbidden fruit out of God's sight. Behind his back. But in the company of Satan instead.

Now God graciously prepares a table us before us. God is demonstrating his great forgiveness, grace, and mercy. Thou we treated him so poorly, he is gracious in return.

Now we again eat in the presence of the enemy of our souls. But how different. In addition to showing us his great love and grace, God is also demonstrating the failure of the plot to separate us from him. Our enemy watched us eat and earn defeat in the garden; now he watches us eat and receive unearned victory at the banquet table.

What is the banquet table?

The banquet table experience is not eating for survival or sustenance for the journey. We did that in the green meadows as sheep. This is the time of celebration. It is a harvest banquet.

For many of us, we are in a time and place where good food is in proliferation, and we are celebrating something almost every week it seems. In ancient Israel at the time of Jesus's ministry, it was not like that for most people. Banquets were very rare. Money had to be saved for months or even years. This banquet table that God prepares for us is a huge deal.

A good harvest was plenty of reason to celebrate and have a feast. We have made it through the paths of righteousness and the valley of darkness. It is a time for celebration. We should enter into the harvest with rejoicing and thanksgiving.

Marriage supper

The banquet table is also a marriage supper:

> Let us rejoice and be glad
>> and give him glory!
> For the wedding of the Lamb has come,
>> and his bride has made herself ready.
> (Revelation 19:7)

Jesus is the Lamb who has become the groom. Jesus went from being the Good Shepherd as protector and provider to our Shepherd guide in the paths to our Deliverer in the valley. Now he is our Divine Lover, the one who wants to be one with us for all of eternity.

Who is the bride? We, the people of God.

We must just give ourselves away to Christ entirely, forsaking all others:

> Whom have I in heaven but you?
>> And earth has nothing I desire besides you.
> (Psalm 73:25)

How do we prepare for the marriage supper?

One of our biggest challenges may be to shift gears from giving and serving to simply receive graciously and without judging. There is nothing else for us to prove. We do not need to impress God. He just desires that we open ourselves to receive. How do we do this?

Celebrate and rejoice in all things

We can develop the habit of giving thanks, celebrating, and rejoicing in all things. This will stand us in good stead for when we attend the marriage celebration. We are in essence practicing, or rehearsing, for this glorious event.

> Rejoice in the Lord always. I will say it again: Rejoice! (Philippians 4:4)

Come empty handed

God wants us. Our heart and soul. Nothing else. Not anything we can bring. Just bring our love, thanks, and praise:

> Come, all you who are thirsty,
> come to the waters;
> and you who have no money,
> come, buy and eat!
> Come, buy wine and milk
> without money and without cost.
> . . .
> Give ear and come to me;
> listen, that you may live. (Isaiah 55:1, 3)

Do not feel unworthy. We are not invited to the banquet because of something we accomplished. Beyond the fact that we are not really worthy and that God does not need our good deeds, the entire effort-achieve-reward system is now done away with. We no longer need to earn anything or prove anything. We can just be. Be in love with Christ.

To illustrate the great compassion and mercy of God, we have the story of David, one of the precursors of Christ. He was mercilessly hunted by King Saul, who was jealous of David's popularity. In ancient times leaders would take revenge on not just their enemies, but all the family of their enemies, showing no mercy. But David had a friend he loved dearly named Jonathon. Jonathon was a son of Saul. When Jonathon perished along with King Saul in battle, this is what David did:

> David asked, "Is there anyone still left of the house of Saul to whom I can show kindness for Jonathan's sake?"

> Now there was a servant of Saul's household named Ziba. They summoned him to appear before David, and the king said to him, "Are you Ziba?"

> "At your service," he replied.

> The king asked, "Is there no one still alive from the house of Saul to whom I can show God's kindness?"

> Ziba answered the king, "There is still a son of Jonathan; he is lame in both feet."

"Where is he?" the king asked.

Ziba answered, "He is at the house of Makir son of Ammiel in Lo Debar."

So King David had him brought from Lo Debar, from the house of Makir son of Ammiel.

When Mephibosheth son of Jonathan, the son of Saul, came to David, he bowed down to pay him honor.

David said, "Mephibosheth!"

"At your service," he replied.

"Don't be afraid," David said to him, "for I will surely show you kindness for the sake of your father Jonathan. I will restore to you all the land that belonged to your grandfather Saul, and you will always eat at my table." (2 Samuel 9:1–7)

David wanted to bless Saul's relative because of Jonathon, in spite of Saul's actions. And in the same way, God our Father wants to bless us because of Jesus, despite our lameness and our weaknesses.

Come with humility

We did not earn or buy God's kindness, grace, and generosity. It is a pure gift. It is also a rare gift, not to be taken lightly.

We remember who we are even as we enter into God's glory:

> For by the grace given me I say to every one of
> you: Do not think of yourself more highly than
> you ought, but rather think of yourself with sober
> judgment, in accordance with the faith God has
> distributed to each of you. (Romans 12:3)

Remember who Jesus invited to the meal on the sabbath? Wee
Zacchaeus. He had climbed the tree to get a brief glimpse of Jesus.
Instead he was invited to join Jesus at the meal. Zacchaeus was
small, and he was a tax collector. Both insignificant and scorned,
yet special in Jesus's eyes:

> Jesus entered Jericho and was passing through. A
> man was there by the name of Zacchaeus; he was
> a chief tax collector and was wealthy. He wanted
> to see who Jesus was, but because he was short he
> could not see over the crowd. So he ran ahead and
> climbed a sycamore-fig tree to see him, since Jesus
> was coming that way.
>
> When Jesus reached the spot, he looked up and
> said to him, "Zacchaeus, come down immediately.
> I must stay at your house today." So he came down
> at once and welcomed him gladly. (Luke 19:1–6)

Receive with grace

In the paths and valley we were asked to work and give and
sacrifice and surrender. Praise and thanks to God, if we have
traveled this far, we did so.

When God gives someone wealth and possessions and the ability to enjoy them, to accept their lot and be happy in their toil, this is a gift of God (Ecclesiastes 5:19).

> *Love bade me welcome; yet my soul drew back,*
> *Guilty of dust and sin.*
> *But quick-eyed Love, observing me grow slack*
> *From my first entrance in,*
> *Drew nearer to me, sweetly questioning*
> *If I lack'd anything.*
> *"A guest," I answer'd, "worthy to be here:"*
> *Love said, 'You shall be he.'*
> *"I, the unkind, ungrateful? Ah, my dear,*
> *I cannot look on Thee."*
> *Love took my hand and smiling did reply,*
> *"Who made the eyes but I?"*
> *"Truth, Lord; but I have marr'd them: let my shame*
> *Go where it doth deserve."*
> *"And know you not," says Love, "Who bore the blame?"*
> *"My dear, then I will serve."*
> *"You must sit down," says Love, "and taste my meat."*
> *So I did sit and eat.*
> —George Herbert, "Love"

Lavish our love on Christ

We need to remember that we are celebrating knowing, truly knowing, Christ. And becoming one with him. Our blessed destiny. God's will.

Remember Mary, the one who greatly loved Jesus?

Jesus came to Bethany . . . Here a dinner was given
in Jesus' honor . . . Then Mary took about a pint
of pure nard, an expensive perfume; she poured
it on Jesus' feet and wiped his feet with her hair.
And the house was filled with the fragrance of the
perfume. (John 12:1–3)

At the banquet, our attention is not on the food. Or our position
at the table. Or our enemies looking on. Or ourselves. It is on our
fellow diner, the Lord Jesus. He is why we are there. He is our
Divine Lover.

> *When blessed Marie wip'd her Saviours feet,*
> *(Whose precepts she had trampled on before)*
> *And wore them for a jewell on her head,*
> *Shewing his steps should be the street,*
> *Wherein she thenceforth evermore*
> *With pensive humblenesse would live and tread*
> *She being stain'd herself, why did she strive*
> *To make him clean, who could not be defil'd?*
> *Why kept she not her tears for her own faults,*
> *And not his feet? Though we could dive*
> *In tears like seas, our sinnes are pil'd*
> *Deeper than they, in words, and works, and thoughts.*
> *Deare soul, she knew who did vouchsafe and deigne*
> *To bear her filth ; and that her sinnes did dash*
> *Ev'n God himself ; wherefore she was not loth,*
> *As she had brought wherewith to stain,*
> *So to bring in wherewith to wash :*
> *And yet in washing one, she washed both.*
> —George Herbert, "Mary Magdalene"

We fix our eyes upon him. We gaze upon him, passing from glory
to glory.

What is it that we are eating and consuming? His very life and love! We know and remember that it is all from him. We now can fully know and receive the fullness of his love and blessing.

Our hearts and souls are entirely open to Christ. Our minds are consumed by knowing his love.

We ask God to empower us that we may "grasp how wide and long and high and deep is the love of Christ, and to know this love that surpasses knowledge—that [we] may be filled to the measure of all the fullness of God" (Ephesians 3:18–19).

> *He caused the floods of infinite tenderness pent up in His Divine Heart to overflow into the soul of His little Spouse.*
> —Therese of Lisieux, *Story of a Soul*

Accept the invitation to the banquet

Everyone is invited to God's feast, but as hard as it is to believe, many refuse the invitation. At one sabbath dinner someone said to Jesus, "Blessed is the one who will eat at the feast in the kingdom of God" (Luke 14:15). And in response Jesus told a story:

> Jesus replied: "A certain man was preparing a great banquet and invited many guests. At the time of the banquet he sent his servant to tell those who had been invited, 'Come, for everything is now ready.'
>
> "But they all alike began to make excuses. The first said, 'I have just bought a field, and I must go and see it. Please excuse me.'

"Another said, 'I have just bought five yoke of oxen, and I'm on my way to try them out. Please excuse me.'

"Still another said, 'I just got married, so I can't come.'

"The servant came back and reported this to his master. Then the owner of the house became angry and ordered his servant, 'Go out quickly into the streets and alleys of the town and bring in the poor, the crippled, the blind and the lame.'

"'Sir,' the servant said, 'what you ordered has been done, but there is still room.'

"Then the master told his servant, 'Go out to the roads and country lanes and compel them to come in, so that my house will be full. I tell you, not one of those who were invited will get a taste of my banquet.'" (vv. 16–18, 24)

What were the excuses? Buying land, buying oxen, getting married. These are not bad things. The invited guests are not busy stealing or getting drunk. They are busy with the affairs of life.

It is easy for us to say that we would never say no to God. But how much time did we make for God today? In the last week? In the last minute?

They are not saying they will never come to the feast. They are only saying that the time is bad for them. So, it is all about priorities. About sacrificing one thing for another.

We can say–Please, God, we want to accept the invitation for the feast that was paid for by untold suffering and death!

Soak in the truth that time with God is always infinitely more beneficial than anything else:

> Better is one day in your courts than a thousand elsewhere; (Psalm 84:10)

What would hold us back from celebrating?

Recall how the prodigal son's older brother refused to celebrate. He was outraged at the grace his father showed his brother:

> Meanwhile, the older son was in the field. When he came near the house, he heard music and dancing. So he called one of the servants and asked him what was going on. "Your brother has come," he replied, "and your father has killed the fattened calf because he has him back safe and sound." The older brother became angry and refused to go in. (Luke 15:25–28)

We must avoid wrong judgment of people and circumstances. Yes, we should work for justice and protect others from predators. But we can do so without impurities in our hearts such as anger, jealousy, and bitterness. To do so keeps us from intimacy and oneness with Christ.

We need to join the celebration with no strings attached. Regardless of how God arranges the celebration, or who is there, we should just rejoice.

Chapter 15

Anointing

Following the banquet, we move to the second part of Psalm 23:5:

> You anoint my head with oil;

Anointing is an ancient tradition whereby people were set aside and commissioned for service as priests and rulers. Other uses of anointing with oil that we will not focus on here include blessing guests and healing the sick.

All the way back when the Israelites escaped from slavery in Egypt, over 1,000 years before Jesus was born, their priests were consecrated for service:

> Take the anointing oil and anoint him by pouring it on his head. (Exodus 29:7)

The priests were from the tribe of the Levites. The kings were taken from other tribes. But Jesus combined being a king and a priest and was accordingly anointed.

Jesus quotes Isaiah in Luke 4, speaking of himself:

> The Spirit of the Lord is on me,
>   because he has anointed me
>   to proclaim good news to the poor.
> He has sent me to proclaim freedom for the prisoners
>   and recovery of sight for the blind,
> to set the oppressed free,
> to proclaim the year of the Lord's favor. (vv. 18–19)

And referring to Jesus in the book of Acts, Luke says:

> . . . God anointed Jesus of Nazareth with the Holy Spirit and power, and . . . he went around doing good and healing all who were under the power of the devil, because God was with him. (Acts 10:38)

Now, God anoints us through Jesus:

> Now it is God who makes both us and you stand firm in Christ. He anointed us, (2 Corinthians 1:21)

> But you have an anointing from the Holy One, and all of you know the truth. (1 John 2:20)

> As for you, the anointing you received from him remains in you, and you do not need anyone to teach you. But as his anointing teaches you about all things and as that anointing is real, not counterfeit—just as it has taught you, remain in him. (1 John 2:27)

As we see from these final few verses, God's plan is to anoint you and me. By doing this he is defining how he sees us, and how he will use us in a powerful way. He is setting us apart and making us his special representatives.

Spend a moment thinking of your various roles and titles in this life. You are a family member, maybe a husband or wife, parent. You may be a student at a particular school. You may have a job with a title or position.

Far above any of these roles and titles in this world, you are anointed by God with a more distinguished and important role in his kingdom.

Are we really to be leaders and priests?

In your outer being, in this life, you may or may not have any sort of leadership position, and you probably do not have the title of priest or minister or pastor.

But this anointing still applies to you and me, because we are referring to something different than a formal title.

If you have come this far on your journey in your inner being, you are crafted for God to use you as his instrument and tool:

> For we are God's handiwork, created in Christ
> Jesus to do good works, which God prepared in
> advance for us to do. (Ephesians 2:10)

This includes leading and ministry. We are anointed, as Christ was, for leadership and for ministry. This is the royal (leadership) priesthood (ministry) referred to here:

> But you are a chosen people, a royal priesthood . . .
> (1 Peter 2:9)

A part of the plan

Our anointing was God's plan from the start.

God commissioned humans to tend the garden and have dominion over the earth:

> The Lord God took the man and put him in the Garden of Eden to work it and take care of it. (Genesis 2:15)
>
> And God said, "Let us make man in our image, after our likeness: and let them have dominion over the fish of the sea, and over the fowl of the air, and over the cattle, and over all the earth, and over every creeping thing that creepeth upon the earth." (Genesis 1:26 KJV)

God clearly intends that humanity should be leaders (have dominion).

Although not quite as direct, it is fair to say that the instructions to care for the garden can also translate into our caring for and ministering to one another. How do we do it? We lead and minister to others, pouring into them what God has poured into us.

In the garden, Adam blamed Eve for the act of disobedience, and Eve in turn blamed the serpent. Then humanity was cast out of the garden and had to struggle to survive. This act of blaming others to save ourselves, along with our need to struggle to survive, brought on our propensity to think only of ourselves and our own interests.

As humanity became more populous and cities were established, we were forced to cooperate to function and flourish. Although we were forced out of self-interest to consider the needs of others, our hearts and souls continued to be primarily focused on self. Even helping others might be done to feel better about oneself.

Now we can reverse this part of the curse by serving and caring about others truly, in our hearts and souls. For the sake of Christ. To become one with him in his caring and compassion.

Why is it necessary to continue leading and ministering?

Even after Christ returns to the earth, it is interesting that we, his people, will rule:

> And they will reign for ever and ever.
> (Revelation 22:5)

Why is there a need to rule if everything is fixed and made perfect? And even if there is a need, why doesn't Jesus do it all himself?

Maybe ultimately it is not really about the functional and practical need to rule and minister. God can take care of all of that himself. Perhaps it is that he wants to share his full nature with us as we become one with him. This nature includes leading and ministering.

It is a bit like when we were in the garden. We were asked to tend and care for the garden, even though God was perfectly capable of doing it himself. But he wanted us to do it so that we could share some of his creative and caring attributes with us. So now we lead and serve to bless others and to become more like Christ.

How should we respond to being anointed for service and leading?

Perhaps you are or have in the past been involved in serving, ministering, helping, or leading. Maybe you already feel anointed by God. How is the anointing at this stage different?

Leadership as we become one with Christ is entirely different. It is the opposite of what it seems. In this life leadership means extending ourselves beyond the self and into the world. Through some combination of people, things, and information we express ourselves. It is really an extension and exercise of our power. It may not take the form of force or coercion. It might be even subtle persuasion or collaboration. And it will typically be done for what we see as good. But still, it is us, self, writ large. It is our being extended and manifested. Just as God is designed to extend and express and manifest. It is one of the ways we want to be like God.

Good counsel was given in Scripture. After James and John asked to sit on the right and on the left of Jesus in glory, the other disciples heard about it and were understandably angry. So,

> Jesus called them together and said, "You know that those who are regarded as rulers of the Gentiles lord it over them, and their high officials exercise authority over them. Not so with you. Instead, whoever wants to become great among you must be your servant, and whoever wants to be first must be slave of all. For even the Son of Man did not come to be served, but to serve,

and to give his life as a ransom for many." (Mark 10:42–45)

Perhaps the most difficult thing to shed is the natural feeling of wanting to "make a difference," "change the world," "save" people and things, consider what we are doing is important. Serving in the past has ultimately been about self even when we thought and meant it to serve God and do it for him and to help others.

This is why God is not instructing us to lead and to minister. He is anointing us to do so. Anointing represents something flowing from the anointer into the anointing. It changes us in our substance.

In other words, it is to be all from him and for him and through him and in him. We are just the broken yet blessed vessels through which the work is done. We may be virtually impervious to the work being accomplished, even while being consumed by intimacy with him, his glory and love and mercy and goodness and compassion and caring:

> I am crucified with Christ: nevertheless I live; yet
> not I, but Christ liveth in me: (Galatians 2:20)

We have disappeared, and now it is Christ living through us. Thinking his thoughts, speaking his words, performing his actions.

> . . . one God and Father of all, who is above all and
> through all and in all. (Ephesians 4:6)

This enables us to allow the gifts and power of God to extend beyond ourselves. We can see ourselves as streams flowing from our inner being to our outer being and into others. We can open our hearts and share our lives with compassion, with mercy, with grace. Encouraging, comforting, interceding, and advocating.

We are no longer agents with channels to God, we have become his channels and expression. We are living epistles. We have become part of his Word spoken out and projected from himself:

> You show that you are a letter from Christ, the result of our ministry, written not with ink but with the Spirit of the living God, not on tablets of stone but on tablets of human hearts. (2 Corinthians 3:3)

What is it like to be a royal priesthood?

Our journey to oneness with Christ has blessed us beyond all measure. Because Chris and us, together as one, love other people, we want to help them on their journeys as well so they can share in this glorious blessing:

> No one lights a lamp and puts it in a place where it will be hidden, or under a bowl. Instead they put it on its stand, so that those who come in may see the light. (Luke 11:33)

> Those who are wise will shine like the brightness of the heavens, and those who lead many to righteousness, like the stars for ever and ever. (Daniel 12:3)

We want to see others healed and delivered. The Apostle Paul speaks of "the authority the Lord gave me for building you up, not for tearing you down" (2 Corinthians 13:10).

Greater leadership

Much has been said about servant leadership. Jesus set the perfect example. It is modelling what is right and then helping others to do it. A great example is when Jesus washed the feet of his disciples. He was their leader, and yet performed the most humble and lowly of services for them. And note he did it when he was most aware of his great power:

> Jesus knew that the Father had put all things under his power, and that he had come from God and was returning to God; so he got up from the meal, took off his outer clothing, and wrapped a towel around his waist. After that, he poured water into a basin and began to wash his disciples' feet, drying them with the towel that was wrapped around him. (John 13:3–5)

If we think about the ministry of Jesus on the earth, we often think about his great acts of service. This is so good and true.

But perhaps there is something even greater. It is that he ministers as he leads in the sense that he grants to us what he first possesses. For example, he granted his peace in the storm. He gives us his knowledge and wisdom. He grants his forgiveness.

Greatest of all, he granted his love, reaching out with an open heart. It is exercising that pure and selfless love that transcends mere words or action. It is filling that deepest need that we may not even be aware of but may remember feeling as a child or feeling in our dreams. Jesus's love is the satisfaction and fulfillment of every need we have ever felt—even the needs that have been corrupted and distorted and send us seeking others things.

This is the great poet Dante Alighieri's Beatrice. According to Dante, in real life he met her only twice, the first when he and she were only nine years old. Although she was a real person, Dante idealized her into the purest form of love he could conceive and contemplate. This is Jesus, the pure love and pure lover.

Ministry is helping others learn and grow in this pure love in their inner being. How do we help them? We can gently and humbly share how we are pursuing our journeys to fulfillment in this divine love, while encouraging them in their own journeys. God can inspire others to desire and envision this oneness in love.

If you want to build a ship, don't drum up the men to
gather wood, divide the work, and give orders. Instead,
teach them to yearn for the vast and endless sea.
—Antoine de Saint-Exupéry

Chapter 16

Our Cup Runs Over

> . . . *my cup overflows.*
> —Psalm 23:5

Up until this point on our journey we have decreased and become nothing so that God could make us something. This was the life of John the Baptist. Here John says it so well, referring to Jesus as people deserted John to join the crowds surrounding Jesus:

> He must become greater; I must become less.
> (John 3:30)

Through our journey we have given up everything. But thanks to God, our sacrifice has not been in vain. Our sacrifice was sown in Christ and now brings forth a great harvest:

> Very truly I tell you, unless a kernel of wheat falls to the ground and dies, it remains only a single seed. But if it dies, it produces many seeds. Anyone who loves their life will lose it, while

anyone who hates their life in this world will keep it for eternal life. (John 12:24–25)

Now our Good Shepherd fills our cup to overflowing.

Abundant waters in scripture

The idea of abundant and overflowing waters is a recurring theme in Scripture.

Abraham sent his servant to find a bride for his son Isaac. Not just any bride, but the one that would bear the line of promise and blessing all the way to the Messiah, Jesus Christ.

Notice how Rebecca was selected as a bride for Isaac:

> She went down to the spring, filled her jar and came up again.
>
> The servant hurried to meet her and said, "Please give me a little water from your jar."
>
> "Drink, my lord," she said, and quickly lowered the jar to her hands and gave him a drink. After she had given him a drink, she said, "I'll draw water for your camels too, until they have had enough to drink." So she quickly emptied her jar into the trough, ran back to the well to draw more water, and drew enough for all his camels. (Genesis 24:16–20)

And this encounter led to a marriage. Now the overflowing cup leads to the selection of the bride of Christ.

Later Jesus had an experience with a well that is strangely similar in certain regards. Jesus was traveling through Samaria and was tired and thirsty when this occurred:

> So he came to a town in Samaria called Sychar, near the plot of ground Jacob had given to his son Joseph. Jacob's well was there, and Jesus, tired as he was from the journey, sat down by the well. It was about noon.
>
> When a Samaritan woman came to draw water, Jesus said to her, "Will you give me a drink?"
>
> The Samaritan woman said to him, "You are a Jew and I am a Samaritan woman. How can you ask me for a drink?"
>
> Jesus answered her, "If you knew the gift of God and who it is that asks you for a drink, you would have asked him and he would have given you living water."
>
> "Sir," the woman said, "you have nothing to draw with and the well is deep. Where can you get this living water? Are you greater than our father Jacob, who gave us the well and drank from it himself, as did also his sons and his livestock?"
>
> Jesus answered, "Everyone who drinks this water will be thirsty again, but whoever drinks the water I give them will never thirst. Indeed, the water I give them will become in them a spring of water welling up to eternal life." (John 4:5–14)

Jesus offers living waters that will well up to eternal life. This is the true spiritual overflowing.

Finally, God lays out the stream flowing from the throne of God in Ezekiel 47. Note how it gets deeper and deeper, even as the drink Jesus mentioned at the well wells up unto eternal life:

> The man [an angel] brought me [the prophet Ezekiel] back to the entrance to the temple, and I saw water coming out from under the threshold of the temple
>
> . . .
>
> As the man went eastward with a measuring line in his hand, he measured off a thousand cubits and then led me through water that was ankle-deep. He measured off another thousand cubits and led me through water that was knee-deep. He measured off another thousand and led me through water that was up to the waist. He measured off another thousand, but now it was a river that I could not cross, because the water had risen and was deep enough to swim in—a river that no one could cross. (Ezekiel 47:1, 3–5)

God promises overflowing waters.

What is the purpose of overflowing living waters?

The living waters generate flourishing gardens in our souls. Our inner being has grown bit by bit throughout our journey, by God's grace, through our work and sacrifice. But now God lavishly overflows us with his grace in our inner being, while we sit and rest.

What can these waters be compared with? Streams in the desert:

> See, I am doing a new thing!
> Now it springs up; do you not perceive it?
> I am making a way in the wilderness
> and streams in the wasteland. (Isaiah 43:19)

What are our hearts and souls overflowing with? The fruit of the Spirit, such as love (1 Thessalonians 3:12). But since this is after the valley, these attributes are greater and purer. It is an experience beyond what we can know or understand.

Looking forward

How can we prepare for this day in our journey, when God causes our cup to overflow? We may feel like our cup is far from overflowing at this present time. We may even feel dry and spent and that such overflowing abundance is remote and will never arrive.

Despite this, we can cultivate a sense not just of sufficiency and contentment but of abundance. Setting our feelings aside, we remember that God is generous and that he lavishes us with his love and blessings:

> His love for you overflows even more . . .
> (2 Corinthians 7:15 VOICE)

> See what great love the Father has lavished on
> us, that we should be called children of God! (1
> John 3:1)

In embracing this we break the inner chains of finiteness.

We currently live in a finite world. A world of boundaries. Of trade-offs. Of limitations. Now these limitations begin to disappear. Our souls break through these boundaries. We no longer compare and judge. There is no longer a world of opposites. Of this and that.

We can even now begin changing our patterns of thinking to embrace the experience of a limitless God, limitless love, limitless goodness.

God offers us even now his Spirit without limit:

> . . . for God gives him the Spirit without limit.
> (John 3:34)

Give it back to God

How should we respond to God's lavishness? All that we receive we shall want to give back to Christ:

> the twenty-four elders fall down before him who
> sits on the throne and worship him who lives for
> ever and ever. They lay their crowns before the
> throne and say:
>
> "You are worthy, our Lord and God,
> to receive glory and honor and power,
> for you created all things,
> and by your will they were created
> and have their being." (Revelation 4:10–11)

As water returns to the sea, God's design is for all to go forth from him and then return to him. It will become a continuous flow. We will be his channels. This is how we become one with him. All flows from God the Father to Christ and then from Christ to us, and now it flows back.

The faster it flows out of us, the faster more flows into us. Ultimately this flow is infinite and eternal. It stopped because we stopped it and made it finite and corrupted it. Now it will be a pure, flowing stream.

Chapter 16

Forever

The last verse of Psalm 23, the outline of our spiritual journey, reads:

> Surely your goodness and love will follow me all
> the days of my life, and I will dwell in the house
> of the LORD forever. (v. 6)

This is when it happens. Oneness. Divine love. The consummation of the divine marriage. The work is done. We are entirely at peace with God. We share all and hold back nothing.

> *And the end of all our exploring*
> *Will be to arrive where we started*
> *And know the place for the first time.*
> —T.S. Eliot, *Four Quartets*

In Christ, our perfect divine love, we are his and he is ours. He is our everything. As the song says, we flow into the oceans of His infinite love. We press forward by giving ourselves up completely in pure ecstasy and rapture.

We must surrender, as he is fully living with us and through us.

How do we prepare for this incredible moment? By continuously cultivating the mindset "I am his and he is mine." Live in anticipation of this state. Know that it is greater than all we can ask or imagine. It is the complete fulfillment of all things.

We should dream about this state. Our eyes should always be on it. We must keep reminding ourselves that it is our ultimate destiny.

It is like the bride and groom who dream of being married and becoming one with another. It is to be our constant desire. Our constant pursuit. It transcends all that we can conceive.

We can cultivate and nurture time with Christ. Just be silent and open and listen, without filtering or judging or constraining. Listen for him to tell you how he loves you. We must give him everything and hold nothing back.

> *for love is as strong as death,*
> *its jealousy unyielding as the grave.*
> *It burns like blazing fire,*
> *like a mighty flame.*
> *Many waters cannot quench love;*
> *rivers cannot sweep it away.*
> —Song of Solomon 8:6–7

We can hope, anticipate, envision, and dream of eternity with Christ, of becoming one with him in perfect love, perfect peace, and perfect joy. Completely and entirely fulfilled and satisfied.

> *Death but the Drift of Eastern Gray,*
> *Dissolving into Dawn away*
> —Emily Dickinson, "Behind Me – dips Eternity"

A death is not the extinguishing of a light,
but the putting out of the lamp
because the dawn has come.
—Rabindranath Tagore

Conclusion

This book is written from one traveler to another who has the desire to follow the path that God has for each of us. By sharing our insights and ideas, by encouraging one another, by opening our hearts to one another, we can succeed in our journey.

I pray that we are the ones who are up for the adventure and committed to enduring and overcoming all adversity, pressing forward, trusting God, and being led by him into his chosen destiny for us. As the Apostle Paul admonishes:

> Run in such a way as to get the prize. (1 Corinthians 9:24)

When we do this, we will arrive at the end of our lives like Paul, able to say, "I have fought the good fight, I have finished the race, I have kept the faith" (2 Timothy 4:7).

We can stay faithful throughout our journey. There will be seasons of plenty and seasons of lean, refreshing and gentle rain followed by what feels like parching desert. There will be times when we feel like we have given up everything and received nothing in return. There will be times when we will feel like turning back. While I know this sounds trite, it is not the end of the story. The longer we are faithful with what we do not yet see or perceive or experience, the greater our reward will be. Do not be discouraged, as the tough times are sometimes the invisible and unseen source of the greatest progress. Never give up.

We look forward to hearing these words from Jesus:

> Well done, good and faithful servant! You have been faithful with a few things; I will put you in charge of many things. Come and share your master's happiness! (Matthew 25:21)

I have committed to pray each day for all who are on their journeys, pressing forward with perseverance. I pray that the thoughts and ideas shared here will be a blessing and a help to my fellow sojourners.

May God bless you and strengthen you and grant you wisdom and love in all things.

End? No, the journey doesn't end here. Death is just another path, one that we all must take. The grey rain-curtain of this world rolls back, and all turns to silver glass, and then you see it.
—J.R.R. Tolkien

Appendix

Famous Journeys from the Bible

Here we look at the journeys of some famous individuals in the Bible. God used each of these persons for his plan for humanity in their time. It is amazing to see that while these people are very different and each of their stories is unique, their journeys all follow God's map (Psalm 23). You are probably familiar with some or all of the stories. A few were mentioned earlier in this book.

These are all individuals who struggled and made mistakes and had weaknesses and failures. And yet they have one thing in common: they kept their faith, persevered, and by God's strength made it successfully to the finish line.

Each story is true, and we can learn from each. God asks us to look at them and be inspired to step out on our journey with courage:

> Therefore, since we are surrounded by such a great
> cloud of witnesses, let us throw off everything that
> hinders and the sin that so easily entangles. And
> let us run with perseverance the race marked out

for us, fixing our eyes on Jesus, the pioneer and perfecter of faith. For the joy set before him he endured the cross, scorning its shame, and sat down at the right hand of the throne of God. Consider him who endured such opposition from sinners, so that you will not grow weary and lose heart. (Hebrews 12:1–3)

Noah

Noah was just nine generations removed from Adam. Noah was a righteous man. The same could not be said for the rest of his generation:

> The LORD saw how great the wickedness of the human race had become on the earth, (Genesis 6:5)

God used Noah powerfully to save humanity and get a fresh start, a do-over of sorts. Here is how his journey worked out.

Phase One: Calling

We do not know much about Noah's younger life. However, we can be fairly confident that Noah grew up being told about God and his goodness, since his great grandfather was Enoch. Enoch "walked faithfully with God; then he was no more, because God took him away" (Genesis 5:24). Enoch lived 300 years after Noah's grandfather, Methuselah was born. The generations were very spread out, but surely Enoch's faith would have impacted Noah greatly. He was provided with a wonderful spiritual heritage.

In addition, he was given a great word. When Noah was born, his father prophesied, "He will comfort us in the labor and painful toil of our hands caused by the ground the Lord has cursed" (Genesis 5:29).

God saw that "the wickedness of man was great in the earth . . . But Noah found favor in the eyes of the Lord" (Genesis 6:5, 8), so God said to him:

> So make yourself an ark. . . I am going to bring floodwaters on the earth to destroy all life under the heavens, every creature that has the breath of life in it. Everything on earth will perish. But I will establish my covenant with you, and you will enter the ark—you and your sons and your wife and your sons' wives with you. (Genesis 6:14, 17–18)

Phase Two: Providing

There were likely no ships in Noah's time and no nautical knowledge. Noah was entirely dependent on God. God gave Noah a very specific blueprint for the ark. Here is a very small part of the instructions: "This is how you are to build it: The ark is to be three hundred cubits long, fifty cubits wide and thirty cubits high." (Genesis 6:15).

Phase Three: Leading

"Noah did everything just as God commanded him" (Genesis 6:22). He had to learn patience, as he likely spent many years in construction with nothing to show for his time and effort in the eyes of the world. He was also undoubtedly subject to great derision from his neighbors.

The day finally came when God instructed Noah and his family to enter the ark. God then sealed them in, down in the dark. Noah and his family disappeared from the earth, and for seven days nothing happened. Then the rain started, and the earth was flooded, while the Ark floated safely on the waters.

Phase Four: Testing

The flood finally began to recede, but it took close to a half a year. We can imagine that supplies were running low and tempers were rising in that small space cut off from the world. God, in his grace and kindness, "remembered Noah and all the wild animals and the livestock that were with him in the ark, and he sent a wind over the earth, and the waters receded." (Genesis 8:1). God gave them hope when Noah sent out a dove: "And the dove came back to him in the evening, and behold, in her mouth was a freshly plucked olive leaf" (v. 11).

Phase Five: Redeeming

The ground dried, and Noah and his family emerged into the bright sunshine and the new world. This was their new life provided by God. They started human life anew, knowing God's faithfulness and promises. God provided a rainbow as a sign that "As long as the earth endures, seedtime and harvest, cold and heat, summer and winter, day and night will never cease." (Genesis 8:22).

Abraham (Abram)

Abraham is considered the father of our faith. God gave him the great promise that led to the Messiah, Jesus Christ, and accordingly to our redemption and reconciliation with God. He lived approximately 4,000 years ago.

Phase One: Calling

We do not know much about his early life, but like Noah, Abraham (originally Abram) had a godly heritage. He was in the line of Shem. Shem was one of Noah's three sons. Shem was considered righteous since he helped cover his father's nakedness after his father drank too much wine. For this, Noah blessed Shem first.

When Abraham was young, he moved with his family to Harran, an ancient city located in modern-day Turkey. Abraham then married Sarah (originally Sarai).

The time came, and God instructed Abraham to depart from Harran with Sarah. God told him, "Go from your country, your people and your father's household to the land I will show you. I will make you into a great nation, and I will bless you. I will make your name great, and you will be a blessing. I will bless those who bless you, and whoever curses you I will curse; and all peoples on earth will be blessed through you" (Genesis 12:1–3).

Phase Two: Providing

God led Abraham and provided for him, including by finally giving him a son, Isaac, through whom the blessing would flow (Genesis 21). God granted Abraham great wealth and possessions and granted him victory against his enemies when he fought to rescue his nephew, Lot (Genesis 14).

Phase Three: Leading

Abraham obeyed God's instructions and ". . . went, as the LORD had told him" (Genesis 12:4). Later God told him, "To your offspring I will give this land" (Genesis 12:7), confirming Abraham's path.

Phase Four: Testing

Now God would seemingly take it all away. He instructed Abraham to take Isaac and sacrifice him on an altar that God would show him. Abraham obeyed by rising early and traveling with Isaac to the site of the sacrifice. Abraham had to act out of faith, and we see his faith in his confidence in telling Isaac that God would provide the sacrifice.

At the last moment God stopped Abraham and said, "Do not lay a hand on the boy . . . Do not do anything to him. Now I know that you fear God, because you have not withheld from me your son, your only son" (Genesis 22:12).

Abraham was willing to give up what he held dearest. All the wonderful promises he had received could have been null and void.

Phase Five: Redeeming

In the end, God spared the life of Isaac and richly blessed Abraham for his faithfulness:

> The angel of the LORD called to Abraham from heaven a second time and said, "I swear by myself, declares the LORD, that because you have done this and have not withheld your son, your only son, I will surely bless you and make your descendants as numerous as the stars in the sky and as the sand on the seashore. Your descendants will take possession of the cities of their enemies, and through your offspring all nations on earth will be blessed, because you have obeyed me."
> (Genesis 22:15–18)

Jacob

Jacob was one of Abraham's grandsons. Although he struggled greatly, he prevailed in the end by God's grace, and the promises of Abraham were said to pass down through him.

Phase One: Calling

Jacob grew up wealthy and knew that God's promise was upon his family. But there was a prophecy from God specifically about him as well. When Rebekah was pregnant with Esau and Jacob, twins (but definitely not identical), she felt a jostling in her womb. Here is what happened:

> So she went to inquire of the Lord.
> The LORD said to her,

"Two nations are in your womb,
and two peoples from within you will be separated;
one people will be stronger than the other,
and the older will serve the younger."

When the time came for her to give birth, there were twin boys in her womb. The first to come out was red, and his whole body was like a hairy garment; so they named him Esau. After this, his brother came out, with his hand grasping Esau's heel; so he was named Jacob. (Genesis 25:22–26)

However, Jacob did not trust God to provide in his way and time. When his father, Isaac, was old and lying on his deathbed, Jacob schemed with his mother to steal his older brother's blessing.

Phase Two: Providing

When Esau found out what Jacob had done, he was furious, and quite capable of violence. Although Esau intended to kill Jacob, God had other plans. God provided an escape and a way for Jacob to learn some lessons the hard way.

Rebekah, hearing Esau's threats, urged Jacob to flee from his home:

Your brother Esau is planning to avenge himself by killing you. Now then, my son, do what I say: Flee at once to my brother Laban in Harran. Stay with him for a while until your brother's fury subsides. When your brother is no longer angry with you and forgets what you did to him, I'll send word for you to come back from there. Why should I lose both of you in one day? (Genesis 27:42–45)

Jacob wisely listened to her advice.

Phase Three: Leading

Jacob arrived and served his uncle Laban for many years. He had many challenges and struggles during this time and had to learn some tough lessons. He ended up marrying two of his uncle's daughters, Rachel and Leah. He loved Rachel but was tricked into marrying Leah first (Genesis 29). He was tricked and deceived much in the way he had tricked and deceived his brother.

What goes around comes around. However, God finally did bless him, and he became very wealthy and had a very large family and huge herds (Genesis 30:43).

Phase Four: Testing

Uncle Laban and his family felt threatened and jealous of Jacob as he observed how Jacob's flocks flourished more than his own:

> Jacob heard that Laban's sons were saying, "Jacob has taken everything our father owned and has gained all this wealth from what belonged to our father." And Jacob noticed that Laban's attitude toward him was not what it had been. (Genesis 31:1–2)

Jacob decided to once again flee a bad situation and leave his uncle and take his family and possessions and return to his original home. But he did not inform his uncle of his departure, and to make matters worse, Rachel secretly stole valuables from her father's house. Discovering their middle-of-the-night flight, Laban and his family and servants pursued and caught up to Jacob and his family. God warned Laban not to harm Jacob, but there was a very tense exchange. Jacob was defensive and embarrassed.

Jacob's next trial would be to meet his brother, Esau, hoping that he would no longer be angry. Jacob instructed his family and servants with their herds and property to go ahead of him and offer great gifts of livestock to Esau as a sort of peace offering. Jacob, in the meantime, stayed alone at Camp Mahanaim.

As he was alone at night in the dark, at risk of losing absolutely everything, including his life, to his brother, this occurred:

> So Jacob was left alone, and a man wrestled with him till daybreak. When the man saw that he could not overpower him, he touched the socket of Jacob's hip so that his hip was wrenched as he wrestled with the man. Then the man said, "Let me go, for it is daybreak."
>
> But Jacob replied, "I will not let you go unless you bless me."
>
> The man asked him, "What is your name?"
>
> "Jacob," he answered.
>
> Then the man said, "Your name will no longer be Jacob, but Israel, because you have struggled with God and with humans and have overcome." (Genesis 32:24–28)

Phase Five: Redeeming

Jacob survived the night and was blessed for it with a new name and identity. He found favor with his brother the next day. He came into a new life back at his home. His eleven sons became the founders of the twelve tribes of Israel (two were Joseph's sons). However, he would suffer deceit and betrayal for many years to come, as some of his sons performed many evil deeds.

Joseph

Joseph was one of Jacob's many children. He was used mightily by God in the divine plan for the Israelites and for our redemption through the Messiah. He, like Jacob, had many struggles in his journey. However, unlike Jacob, perhaps we may think of him more as an innocent victim, someone targeted by those who were jealous of him. In this way he is much more like Jesus. And, like Jesus, he had a tremendous capacity to forgive those who wronged him.

Phase One: Calling

Joseph's mother was Rachel, Jacob's favorite wife. Joseph was therefore very favored as a child and very well provided for. Jacob even gave Joseph a special gift: a coat or garment of many colors. Also, God gave Joseph a special prophetic blessing through a dream. However, unfortunately for Joseph, he told his brothers about it. They were not happy:

> Listen to this dream I had: We were binding
> sheaves of grain out in the field when suddenly my
> sheaf rose and stood upright, while your sheaves

gathered around mine and bowed down to it. (Genesis 37:6–7)

Phase Two: Providing

As a result of his special treatment and Joseph's gloating over his dream, Joseph's brothers became very envious. When Joseph was sent out to the fields by his father to check on his brothers, his brothers grabbed him and threw him into a dry well. Most of his brothers wanted to leave him to die. But God had other plans and sent some travelers who would take Joseph for their own purposes. Here is how it happened:

> So Joseph went after his brothers and found them near Dothan. But they saw him in the distance, and before he reached them, they plotted to kill him.
>
> "Here comes that dreamer!" they said to each other. "Come now, let's kill him and throw him into one of these cisterns and say that a ferocious animal devoured him. Then we'll see what comes of his dreams."
>
> When Reuben heard this, he tried to rescue him from their hands. "Let's not take his life," he said. "Don't shed any blood. Throw him into this cistern here in the wilderness, but don't lay a hand on him." Reuben said this to rescue him from them and take him back to his father.
>
> So when Joseph came to his brothers, they stripped him of his robe—the ornate robe he was

wearing— and they took him and threw him into the cistern. The cistern was empty; there was no water in it.

As they sat down to eat their meal, they looked up and saw a caravan of Ishmaelites coming from Gilead. Their camels were loaded with spices, balm and myrrh, and they were on their way to take them down to Egypt.

Judah said to his brothers, "What will we gain if we kill our brother and cover up his blood? Come, let's sell him to the Ishmaelites and not lay our hands on him; after all, he is our brother, our own flesh and blood." His brothers agreed.

So when the Midianite merchants came by, his brothers pulled Joseph up out of the cistern and sold him for twenty shekels of silver to the Ishmaelites, who took him to Egypt. (Genesis 37:17–28)

This was the decision that sent Joseph on his journey.

Phase Three: Leading

Joseph served as a slave faithfully for many years in Egypt. He served a man named Potiphar, the captain of the guard to the pharaoh. He learned humility and how it felt to be the least and to do the most menial of tasks. He also learned faithfulness and longsuffering and felt how it was to be mistreated.

Phase Four: Testing

As if things couldn't get any worse, Joseph learned how it felt to be betrayed. Potiphar's wife made advances on him, and when he refused them, she accused him of sexual assault. Potiphar then had him thrown in prison. He disappeared behind the prison walls and into a dark dungeon, with no expectation of ever being released. Joseph had every reason to believe that his life was over. Instead of giving up, though, he led and served the other prisoners faithfully in prison by the prompting of God.

Phase Five: Redeeming

Joseph's faithful service to others in prison led him to his release. The pharaoh's cupbearer and baker somehow offended their master, so the pharaoh had them thrown into the same prison with Joseph. As Joseph served them faithfully, they each had a dream. God empowered Joseph to interpret the dreams. He explained to the cupbearer that he would be restored, while the baker would lose his life. This came to pass. The cupbearer promised to remember Joseph in prison and help him, but promptly forgot for two years until one day pharaoh had a dream. The cupbearer then remembered Joseph and told the pharaoh about him. Joseph was called and correctly interpreted his dream of the future—Egypt would experience seven years of plenty followed by seven years of poor harvests.

In brief, God blessed Joseph abundantly and gave him a new life. He was promoted to prime minister of Egypt, and he reconciled with his brothers in a very powerful way and brought them and his father Jacob to Egypt, where they settled and were allowed to flourish and grow into a very sizeable people group. This is what he said to his brothers:

You intended to harm me, but God intended it for good. . . (Genesis 50:20 ESV)

Moses

Moses lived at the time when the Israelites lived in Egypt as slaves, greatly oppressed and mistreated. By a trick of fate, or rather God's design, he could have lived in affluence and comfort and luxury in pharaoh's palace. Yet instead he chose to be counted among the Israelites, and struggled mightily for their deliverance and freedom. In this way he was much like Jesus, who "made himself nothing by taking the very nature of a servant . . ." (Philippians 2:7).

Phase One: Calling

God chose Moses as his instrument to deliver the Israelites from bondage in Egypt and bring them to the land promised to Abraham centuries previously.

For close to 400 years following the time of Joseph, the Israelites dwelled in Egypt. Egyptian leaders began to worry as the Israelites grew in number and wealth. Egyptian pharaohs began to enslave and oppress the Israelites. The Egyptians then decided to kill Israelite male babies in an effort to limit their population. Moses was an Israelite baby born into this situation. Perceiving the great risk, Moses's family hid him in a little basket and sent the basket floating on the Nile River. God had plans for Moses and so arranged that Pharaoh's daughter would find the little baby and take pity on him. She raised Moses in pharaoh's court in wealth and luxury.

One day when Moses was in the fields, he observed an Egyptian taskmaster mistreating one of Moses's fellow Hebrews. In his rage, Moses murdered the Egyptian. The next day he realized his action had been observed. He fled to Midian, where he lived in exile for forty years and married and had a family (Exodus 2:11–15).

Then God came to him and called to him in dramatic fashion, speaking from a bush that was ablaze with fire and yet not consumed. God presented Moses with the mission of returning to Egypt, confronting the pharaoh, and leading the Israelites out of Egypt and on a journey to the Promised Land (Exodus 3). Talk about a tough job assignment!

Phase Two: Providing

Moses argued with God and received several promises of help before agreeing to serve in this mission. God promised Moses, "I will be with you. And this will be the sign to you that it is I who have sent you: When you have brought the people out of Egypt, you will worship God on this mountain." (Exodus 3:12). He also promised:

> But I know that the king of Egypt will not let you go unless a mighty hand compels him. So I will stretch out my hand and strike the Egyptians with all the wonders that I will perform among them. After that, he will let you go.
>
> "And I will make the Egyptians favorably disposed toward this people, so that when you leave you will not go empty-handed. Every woman is to ask her neighbor and any woman living in her house for

articles of silver and gold and for clothing, which you will put on your sons and daughters. And so you will plunder the Egyptians." (vv. 19–22)

God was faithful to these promises.

Phase Three: Leading

Just as God said, Pharaoh was resistant when Moses and his brother Aaron visited him. God directed Moses each step of the way, telling him what to say and do, as he performed many powerful signs and sent plagues on Egypt. Only after Egypt suffered from ten plagues and lost their firstborn sons to death, including Pharaoh's son, did Pharaoh finally agree to allow the Israelites to go.

Phase Four: Testing

Then, typical of Pharaoh, he changed his mind and chased after the Israelites with his army of war chariots. The Israelites, defenseless without weapons, were pinned against the Red Sea, the sea in front of them, the enemy behind them. Here is what happened:

> Then the LORD said to Moses, "Why are you crying out to me? Tell the Israelites to move on. Raise your staff and stretch out your hand over the sea to divide the water so that the Israelites can go through the sea on dry ground. I will harden the hearts of the Egyptians so that they will go in after them. And I will gain glory through Pharaoh and all his army, through his chariots and his

horsemen. The Egyptians will know that I am the Lord when I gain glory through Pharaoh, his chariots and his horsemen."

Then the angel of God, who had been traveling in front of Israel's army, withdrew and went behind them. The pillar of cloud also moved from in front and stood behind them, coming between the armies of Egypt and Israel. Throughout the night the cloud brought darkness to the one side and light to the other side; so neither went near the other all night long.

Then Moses stretched out his hand over the sea, and all that night the Lord drove the sea back with a strong east wind and turned it into dry land. The waters were divided, and the Israelites went through the sea on dry ground, with a wall of water on their right and on their left. (Exodus 14:15–22)

Moses and the Israelites marched down into the sea, with no guarantees that the sea would not swallow them. They put their lives on the line, knowing that they probably could have returned to Egypt and resumed their lives (the Egyptians would have been angry and would certainly have killed Moses and Aaron but needed the free labor).

Phase Five: Redeeming

The Israelites were free and on the way to the Promised Land. They had many challenges ahead of them and unfortunately failed to be faithful on their journey. Yet they as a nation would be saved and enter the Promised Land.

Ruth

Ruth was a gentile from Moab. God chose her and pulled her from obscurity and used her powerfully to further the lineage leading to King David and to Jesus. Her mother-in-law, Naomi, served as her guide, even as the Holy Spirit does for us today. Ruth's faith in following this good counsel, her extreme courage, and her decision to throw her future and destiny entirely into the hands of her kinsman redeemer made it possible.

Phase One: Calling

During a famine in Israel, a group of Jews emigrated to Moab. Ruth married one of those Jewish men, who died at a young age, leaving Ruth stuck as a young widow. However, God provided her mother-in-law, Naomi, to love her and help her.

When Naomi prepared to return to Israel after the death of her husband and her two sons, she urged Ruth to return to her people in Moab. Ruth had a decision to make. Here is what she said to her mother-in-law:

> Don't urge me to leave you or to turn back from you. Where you go I will go, and where you stay I will stay. Your people will be my people and your God my God. Where you die I will die, and there I will be buried. May the Lord deal with me, be it ever so severely, if even death separates you and me. (Ruth 1:16–17)

What great faithfulness and determination!

Phase Two : Providing

Naomi provided support to Ruth throughout her journey and beyond.

Phase Three: Leading

Naomi and Ruth traveled to Naomi's hometown, Bethlehem. They were destitute, with no money, no property, and no close family or friends. Thanks to God, Naomi remembered that she had a distant relative on her husband's side, a man of standing from the clan of Elimelek, whose name was Boaz (Ruth 2:1). She suggested that they (she and Ruth) go to his land and glean from the fields (Old Testament Law required that landowners allow the poor to glean, or pick up leftovers after harvest, from the fields). Ruth humbled herself and worked hard in the fields gathering the little grain left on the ground.

In God's timing, Boaz showed up, noticed Ruth, and showed Ruth kindness. He showed her how to best find the grain, ensured she could get water, and asked her to glean only in his fields where she would be safe and provided for (Ruth 2:8–9).

Phase Four: Testing

Ruth put everything on the line and decided to act very boldly, casting herself on the mercy of her kinsman. In ancient times, servants would lie at the feet of their masters. Ruth humbled herself by lying down at his feet. Here is what Ruth did, following Naomi's recommendation:

So she went down to the threshing floor and did everything her mother-in-law told her to do. When Boaz had finished eating and drinking and was in good spirits, he went over to lie down at the far end of the grain pile. Ruth approached quietly, uncovered his feet and lay down. In the middle of the night something startled the man; he turned—and there was a woman lying at his feet!

"Who are you?" he asked.

"I am your servant Ruth," she said. "Spread the corner of your garment over me, since you are a guardian-redeemer of our family." (Ruth 3:6–9)

If she had been spurned by Boaz she would have been disgraced and as a foreigner, probably not welcome anywhere.

Phase Five: Redeeming

Boaz graciously accepted Ruth and redeemed her (purchased her back from the claims of another relative) and even married her. God lifted her up and gave her a new life, and she became the great-grandmother of King David and in the line of Jesus, the Messiah!

Jonah

Jonah lived in Israel around the eighth century BC. Jonah was very prominent and distinguished as a recognized prophet of God, and God's favor was upon him.

Phase One: Calling

God instructed Jonah to travel to Nineveh and give the people God's warning to repent (Jonah 1:2). Nineveh, the capital of the powerful empire of Neo-Assyria, was known to be extremely evil and cruel, and a prophet in Israel would not want anything to do with them.

Jonah made the decision not to obey God. Instead, he decided to head in the opposite direction. He boarded a ship headed for Tarshish (possibly located in modern-day Spain).

Phase Two: Providing

God decided to rescue Jonah from himself in a very interesting way. God sent a storm that would extract Jonah from the ship and get him heading back in the direction of Nineveh.

Phase Three: Leading

Jonah had to learn submission and obedience. As the ship floundered in the storm, Jonah finally decided to humble himself and place himself in God's will. He cried out to the crew:

> "Pick me up and throw me into the sea," he replied, "and it will become calm. I know that it is my fault that this great storm has come upon you." (Jonah 1:12)

Jonah was ready to sacrifice his own life to save the sailors. He was thrown into the sea and sank quickly under the waves.

Phase Four: Testing

A huge fish swallowed Jonah, and he remained in the belly of the fish three days and three nights (Jonah 1:17). Jonah cried out to God in his distress. The fish then vomited Jonah onto dry land.

Phase Five: Redeeming

Jonah finally submitted and preached repentance to Nineveh. By God's grace the Ninevites repented and they and their city were saved from death and destruction.

Jesus

Jesus, as the Son of God, is far above all humans. However, we can see that his journey on earth does indeed fit God's map.

Phase One: Calling

Jesus knew his calling very early on. When his parents found him in the temple at age twelve, he said to them, ""Why were you searching for me?" he asked. "Didn't you know I had to be in my Father's house?" (Luke 2:49). Later, when Jesus was baptized in the Jordan River by John, God the Father spoke to him as he rose up out of the water and said, "This is my beloved Son, with whom I am well pleased" (Luke 3:22). Jesus then began his earthly ministry.

Phase Two: Providing

God the Father provided Jesus with a loving earthly family and a stable home in Nazareth, where he "grew in wisdom and stature" (Luke 2:52). Jesus was given disciples and friends who loved him.

Phase Three: Leading

Jesus was always serving the Father. Jesus said, "For I have come down from heaven not to do my will but to do the will of him who sent me." (John 6:38) and "but he comes so that the world may learn that I love the Father and do exactly what my Father has commanded me." (John 14:31). He spent his time praying and teaching, healing, and loving people.

Phase Four: Testing

Jesus was tested by his trial and crucifixion, but the worst test was arguably how he felt when he spoke these words from the cross: About three in the afternoon Jesus cried out in a loud voice, "Eli, Eli,[a] lema sabachthani?" (which means "My God, my God, why have you forsaken me?") (Matthew 27:46).

Phase Five: Redeeming

Jesus rose from the dead on the third day and ascended to heaven. He has paid for our sins. Now he offers a journey to become one with him in divine love.

Paul (Saul of Tarsus)

Paul of Tarsus grew up as a Hebrew among Hebrews. He says about himself:

> I am a Jew, born in Tarsus of Cilicia, but brought up in this city. I studied under Gamaliel and was thoroughly trained in the law of our ancestors. I was just as zealous for God as any of you are today. (Acts 22:3)

Paul was educated, a prominent Jew, and a Roman citizen due to where he was born.

The Apostle Paul did more than anyone to establish and shape the New Testament church in the world of gentiles. His influence cannot be overstated.

Phase One: Calling

Paul was traveling to Damascus (the capital of modern-day Syria) when:

> suddenly a light from heaven flashed around him. He fell to the ground and heard a voice say to him, "Saul, Saul, why do you persecute me?"
>
> "Who are you, Lord?" Saul asked.
>
> "I am Jesus, whom you are persecuting," he replied. "Now get up and go into the city, and you will be told what you must do."

The men traveling with Saul stood there speechless; they heard the sound but did not see anyone. Saul got up from the ground, but when he opened his eyes he could see nothing. So they led him by the hand into Damascus. For three days he was blind, and did not eat or drink anything. (Acts 9:3–9)

Phase Two: Providing

God directed a disciple by the name of Ananias to go to Paul and help him. God restored Paul's physical vision and provided him with a spiritual vision to preach the gospel (Acts 9:10–19).

Paul made a decision then and there to believe and follow Jesus. He "grew more and more powerful" (Acts 9:22).

Phase Three: Leading

Paul went to Arabia for three years to seek God. Then he spent many years traveling from city to city establishing and building churches (fellowships) in each city throughout the Greek world (including modern-day Turkey and Macedonia as well as Greece). God led him and instructed and guided him throughout all of his travels.

Phase Four: Testing

Paul was brought up on charges based on his faith, so as a Roman citizen he appealed to Caesar and was shipped to Rome and imprisoned. He wrote many of his epistles while imprisoned in Rome and had many visitors.

Phase Five: Redeeming

Near the end of his life, Paul said:

> For I am already being poured out like a drink offering, and the time for my departure is near. I have fought the good fight, I have finished the race, I have kept the faith. Now there is in store for me the crown of righteousness, which the Lord, the righteous Judge, will award to me on that day—and not only to me, but also to all who have longed for his appearing. (2 Timothy 4:6–8)

The churches founded by Paul struggled but ultimately spread Christianity far and wide. Certainly God used his ministry powerfully.

What can we learn from these examples? These examples should encourage us and inspire us to follow and persevere on our journey.

Printed in the United States
By Bookmasters